WRITING FOR PUBLICATION

FOR
PUBLICATION

Clarkson N. Potter

1817
Harper & Row, Publishers, New York
Grand Rapids, Philadelphia, St. Louis, San Francisco
London, Singapore, Sydney, Tokyo, Toronto

FIRST EDITION

Designed by Karen Savary

Library of Congress Cataloging-in-Publication Data

Potter, Clarkson N.
   Writing for publication/Clarkson N. Potter.—1st ed.
      p.   cm.
   Includes bibliographical references.
   ISBN 0-06-016217-1
   1. Authorship.   I. Title.
PN145.P6   1990
808'.02—dc20   89–45703

90 91 92 93 94 CC/RRD 10 9 8 7 6 5 4 3 2 1

This book is for
Howard, Christian, Margaretta, and Edward.

CONTENTS

PREFACE

THIS IS A BOOK about how to become competent. It will not teach you how to write a best-seller or win a Nobel Prize, and it cannot give you talent that isn't there. What it can do, and what it aims to do, is to teach anyone who can write at all how to write better—and by "better" I mean having your writing achieve a level that could be called publishable.

In most writing courses the student reads the work of famous writers, people whose very names conjure up an image of brilliance, fame, success, and enduring value. Few students have the natural talent to emulate, let alone surpass, such lofty models, and as a result they are often not helped very much by such studies and may find themselves deeply discouraged when they compare what they do to what they are asked to read. What they are not told and what they should realize is that most published books and magazine articles do not themselves live up to the best models—that the vast majority of what is published is merely competent. What this means is that most working writers are not great stylists either and have no expectation of much recognition *as a writer*. They write for other reasons—to inform, to persuade, to entertain. What they want, and what they achieve, is writing that serves their other purpose, and this is realized by competence and a professional attitude. I have published dozens of very good books that have done very well in the marketplace that were written by very ordinary writers who could never make the slightest claim to being noticed as being a particularly good writer as such. I have even published successful books that were actually not very well written at all, but succeeded because what they related was information that people wanted; they worked. Biography, for example, is often written without much flair, but because we want to know the story of the person being written about, we may well put up with a plodding exposition. The point is that I think anyone who is willing to work, think a little, and practice a lot can become a publishable writer. Achieving competence, however, is by no means a trivial or instantly attainable goal. It is a worthy goal, and, if ever achieved, a highly satisfying one. This book is intended to show the way to attaining it.

A NOTE ON METHOD

IN SOME SECTIONS OF THIS BOOK the method will not only be the expected one of using examples to demonstrate the point, but will also be the comparative method of showing *good, better,* and *best.*

Years ago when I published antiques guides we found out that what people wanted were books that could tell them the value of a piece they had. To do this they would compare what they saw in front of them with the example illustrated in a book. The pieces in books, of course, were those that had been so highly regarded that they were in museums or outstanding private collections—never the run-of-the-mill sort of thing that the average collector would find himself owning. Thus many of the expensive books that we published really were of limited interest. What they wanted was a book called *Fine Points of Furniture,* which showed at least three examples of every sort of piece. If it was, say, Windsor armchairs, there would be several pictures, showing and analyzing different examples of the type and explaining why one would be thought good, another better, and the most refined the best. This book had an extraordinary life because it was useful in spite of its being itself poorly organized, badly designed, and indifferently printed. It *showed* by comparison what to look for and *why* different examples brought different judgments. It thus offered something that no other book did, which was a rational and understandable way of rating any given object that was at all similar to the things shown in the book.

Now, it may seem that antique furniture and writing have little in common, but to think that would be to overlook what we care about, which is a way to rate, compare, and judge a work of art. Beautiful furniture is now well understood to be great art, at least at times. Good writing is also great art at times. Workaday furniture and workaday writing may not be regarded as art, but to know that we have to make an aesthetic judgment, and to make that judgment requires some sense of style, proportion, harmony, and effectiveness. Thus the *method* of arriving at a judgment can be and, in fact, is the same.

In what follows, then, I have adopted the practice of starting with an example that can loosely be labeled *good,* always, of course, from a published work and often from a well-known work. This is followed by a piece that I think is better, and together with it will be why I think it deserves that label. Then there will be an example of what seems to be the best of its kind. Most of the examples will be from well-known books written by famous writers, but even with these pieces, there is every reason to look at them critically and try to find out for ourselves why they are so highly regarded. Contemplating the very finest may be the pleasure of the aesthete, but comparing the workmanlike is surely the path of the serious student. Since, in this world, we are all students, it is their path that I have chosen to follow.

WRITING FOR PUBLICATION

LEARNING TO WRITE

CAN I TEACH YOU HOW TO WRITE? No. Can you learn to write? Yes. It is perhaps a paradox that writing cannot be taught but can be learned, but that is the plain truth of the matter, and so what will concern us here is just how you can teach yourself to write.

In the first place nothing can be accomplished unless you set yourself a clear and attainable goal. That goal should be to become good enough at writing to produce publishable material. You should not set yourself to rival Tolstoy but only to move from whatever level you have now attained to the level of a professional. If you can write at all—and you can if you can write a letter home when you take a trip—then you are already at some comprehensible level as you start this book and as you contemplate learning to write better.

When I teach a class I always have a few students who say that they don't know how to write at all. But of course they do know how to write. What they really mean is that they don't feel that what they do is worth showing someone else, that they are ashamed of how awkward they are, how strained and inarticulate. If you were to ask them to write down the steps that are necessary to take in order to start a car they would be perfectly capable of putting them down. They wouldn't consider that writing, though, so they think

1

they "can't write." To this attitude I say nonsense. You already are far better equipped than you realize. You have a familiarity with the most expressive, powerful and subtle language that man has ever used. English, largely because it is an amalgamation of several different root languages, has always been open to new words and expressions and hence expands constantly. It is accommodating and flexible in a way that, say, French, is not. It has far more words available for use than other languages and is not constraining in its syntax and structure. It is also rapidly becoming the universal language of educated people over the globe. If you use English as your native language you already have at hand a basic knowledge of its use, and so your real problem is not learning how to write at all, but learning how to write more effectively.

To learn to write you must do two things, practice and compare. They are basic and absolute necessities, and we shall have a closer look at each of them.

The first rule is practice. For a writer to become publishable he needs to do the same thing as does a musician who wishes to play in Carnegie Hall—practice, practice, practice. There is no substitute for it, and so the only question is how to set yourself up to do it. To this end I always say that a set routine is essential. The reason so many people fail at some worthy effort at self-improvement is that they don't stay with it. They get all enthusiastic about some enterprise and launch themselves into a full routine of, say, exercise, and then discover that it is hard and boring work and before they know it, they start skipping the sessions and soon discover that all their good intentions have produced little or nothing.

To avoid this all-too-often-repeated outcome, set yourself modest routines. As we shall see in the next chapter, I advocate starting a diary largely for the reason that it gets you in the habit of writing every day, but even if that doesn't appeal to you, you must decide to adopt a routine— any routine—and set yourself to produce a certain amount of work in a regular way. It should be noted that I don't think that setting aside a regular time—say a day a week or whatever is necessarily the only way to do it. The proper way to do it is to set a goal of a certain number of words or pages that you agree with yourself that you will complete every week or every month. Learning to write well is not some simple matter like improving the size of your quadriceps, and thus you should not expect to measure your progress in days and weeks, but more likely by months and years. The way to meet a goal is to set one that is modest and that you feel sure you can attain. If you were to say to yourself that you intended to write a short story a week, you might get to three or four, but by the time you got to the seventh or tenth week it would have become a terrible chore, and you would probably stop doing it altogether. Suppose you set yourself the goal of three stories in a year. Could you do that? In all probability you could—and because it would be an attainable goal you would be both willing and able to take some real care with each one—so the result might please you quite a bit. The lesson, then, is to practice, but to do so within what you know you can sustain.

The first corollary to the rule of practice is that it requires a routine to be successful. Even if you have adopted the goal of three short stories a year, they will not get written unless you do something like set aside every second Wednesday afternoon for writing. If you are starting and don't yet have established habits of work, one good way to get into it is to enroll in a course. I teach a course in writing and almost all my students take the course because they know that they aren't going to get started at writing unless made to. The class does several things, but the most important is to make the student actually write every week. If people ask me whether writing courses do any good, my answer is that yes, they do a lot of good. If people say to me, well, we live so far from a university that there's no way we could get to a course, or, gee, I don't have enough money to afford something as formal as a course, then I say to them that all that shows is that you don't care enough about it to make any effort. There is almost no city so small that it does not have some institution of learning nearby that offers extension courses, and I think that with only small effort almost anyone can find a course that is close enough and priced reasonably enough for them to take.

A course will serve to get you started, establish a routine, and give you some sense of where you stand in relation to others like yourself. For those reasons I always advocate taking a course no matter who is teaching it. The truth is that big-name people usually care far less for their pupils than the people who have little or no public reputation, so if the course you find is given in an obscure institution by some unknown writer, so much the better. You are taking it for your own reasons, not to be touched by the famous and successful, so what you should be interested in is not them, but you.

The second rule is comparison. By this I mean that you must have a critic and you must not try and learn alone. Obviously one of the reasons you take a course is to get a reading from a professional, and clearly that is all to the good, but you should never make the mistake of thinking that only a professional can criticize your work in a constructive way. One of the first things I learned when I started teaching courses was that the students—who were mostly housewives in their forties and fifties—had no trouble telling whether another student was improving or not. You need only consider yourself in thinking about this. If you can tell that one piece of writing is better than another piece of writing, then you can also tell whether something written by a friend is more or less effective than some other piece written by the same friend. You can think, for example, of letters from a friend or from a child—some are clearly better than others. Without analyzing them you just know right away when one letter is more interesting, more satisfying, then another. And so it is with something a friend writes for a course. And so it is with your own writing.

What this means is that whether or not you take a writing course, if you embark on improving your writing you must at the same time enlist the help of a friend whose judgment you trust. If you know someone else who is also trying to learn to write, then the two of you should become critics for each other. If not, then take a course. There you can meet people who are doing the same thing you are and although they are friendly they are not exactly friends and you can thus hope to establish a more or less professional relationship with someone you meet there. In any case it is perhaps best to pick someone who is not too close to you, someone who you know well enough to work with but don't see every day. A touch of formality will not hurt since, after all, you expect to get frank reports and you intend to give them as well. If your counterpart is *not* showing any improvement in some new piece you are only hurting her and yourself if you fail to point this out. In any case, the rule of comparison is an absolute. You cannot expect to improve alone no matter how much you turn out. Writing is nothing but communication, and that means there is a sender and a receiver; if you write to be the sender but there isn't any receiver, then you might as well be writing messages that are put in bottles and dropped into the outgoing tide. Writing is for reading—so find a reader, and listen carefully to what the reader says. Those, then, are the two great rules of learning to write—practice and compare. We shall now turn to some lesser but still important matters.

In the first place, don't bother with rewriting. It is a mistake to think that a piece of writing can be made perfect by rewriting and extensive revision. Some people assume that there exists a piece that can be thought of as perfect, but I myself would never admit that. I don't think there really is anything that you can point to and say with any security "this is perfect," and if there were, even then the chances that you can attain such a level are small. The natural talent that you have will take a piece to a certain level—whatever it is. Hard revision may enable you to improve a piece by ten percent, or some little bit, however you measure it. I have worked with writers for thirty-five years and have yet to meet one who could improve his prose to any significant degree by doing lengthy revisions. A little bit of polish here and there, a few corrections, the deletion of an awkward passage, all these may well improve a piece, but they are really editing and not fundamental. In addition they are only necessary for a finished piece that will in fact be published. When you are still in the learning and improving stage revision only slows you down and keeps you from turning out more copy, which is what you should be doing. Clearly you should edit and polish a piece, but if you are so dissatisfied with it that you contemplate revising it, then my advice is to scrap the piece entirely and rewrite the whole thing. At the early stages of your learning, and even in later ones, your goal should be to turn out copy in a regular way that is as good as you can make it. Revisions do not teach you much, but writing a new piece does, so just keep going.

In the next place I would remind the student to set a goal of becoming the master of a small field rather than a modest practitioner in many. The rule is—master a small field and then branch out. Once again, it hardly matters what the field may be. It could be anything from training manuals to poetry, although most people choose reportage, short stories or short memoirs. For instruction purposes I recommend the short memoir, since it requires no research and can be launched upon at once. It also has the advantage that in writing it one is likely to have fun. It should be an easy and familiar thing to do, and setting out to write a short memoir should put one in a good mood. Remember that one of my basic rules for life is that if it isn't fun, the hell with it. I don't think that you ever learn to do something well if you hate doing it. I remember John Madden commenting on a football player who had just caught a pass and then had been hit by two defensive backs with particular viciousness. Amazingly, the guy got up grinning, and Madden said, "See! He's got a big grin on his face! He loves it! He loves the game! He doesn't care that he took such a lick! He loves the game and that's why he plays it so well." There's a lesson in that. If you don't like what you're doing you probably won't do it well. The feeling of satisfaction that writing should give you is much easier to attain if you are in a field where you know what you are doing, feel comfortable, and can aspire to know and control.

Next, remember that you have to stay with it. Never give up. Never let yourself get discouraged. Never walk away from the job until it is done. Never stop trying to improve. Oh, I know that these are easy exhortations to put on a page, and that you may respond to them with a sure, sure, we know about that. But it is true that the people who are persistent are the ones who succeed. When I was in college I ran a literary magazine and it was remarkable that at the time we had some real talents in the student body. Several of the young writers I published later went on to significant careers as editors, writers and as teachers, and their talent and dedication to their craft were quite evident even then. There was one student who kept trying to get me to run one of his short stories, but I felt then—as I do now—that he was a lousy writer who would never make it and I always turned him down. Well, he wouldn't take no for an answer and went to New York, took a job as a soda jerk (there were still soda jerks in those days), and wrote at night. It took him twenty years to write something a publisher would take, but he finally did it. I still thought it was lousy, but the book made a lot of money.

The publishing business is full of stories of people who had to go on for years before being recognized or of being turned down by twenty publishers before finding one who said yes. All these stories are tributes to persistence. For success in writing, as in so many other things in life, a relentless drive and an inexhaustible energy will take you far, farther even than mere talent. Even a great gift will get nowhere unless it is harnessed to a will to work. So remember that if you work hard enough and long enough and knock on enough doors, eventually one will indeed open.

Finally, of course, I advise students to read a lot. If you want to write, presumably you also like to read. Do a lot of it, and do it in the field in which you hope to excel yourself. If what you are working on has a formal structure, then you should analyze other people's work to see how they handle it, but I feel that to try and reduce things to formulas is often a mistake. Most writers find out how to do it by a sort of osmotic process. Somehow it subconsciously infuses itself into their brains, as they get used to it. Too much analysis and too much self-consciousness seems to inhibit good writing. Almost all the good writers I know cannot tell me just how they do it. Even when a good writer is working within a very strict formula—as one would be in writing a detective novel—still he seems to keep the formula somewhere outside his consciousness. Somehow once a deep knowledge of a field is established in the brain, following the pattern becomes second nature.

None of this is to imply that you should *not* analyze what you read. You should, especially at the start, when you are not entirely sure how things work. It is well to remember that technical competence is always the first requirement of art, and familiarity with your own field is the first necessity for competence. Besides, it should be fun.

These, then, are the basic things you need to know about writing and learning to write. Your aim is to become professional and to write well enough to be published. In the following chapters we shall see how various writers have accomplished that aim in their chosen fields.

Writing

TO

REMEMBER

DIARIES AND JOURNALS

KEEPING A DIARY OR A JOURNAL is not writing for publication, and yet I advise anyone who wants to learn how to write for publication to keep one or the other. The reason, as I have said, is that it gets one used to writing without pressure. A diary is kept for yourself and you don't really expect to see it in print, so you can say anything that comes to your heart even if it is libelous, blasphemous, or obscene—which is, of course, what most of us think much of the time. But keeping a diary has a couple of subtle effects that I regard as highly beneficial. If you do keep a diary you are forced to think of something that is worth saying, even if it is only to yourself. It also forces you to consider what you do every day, to look inward at your own mind and its response to the everyday world, and this has the general effect of making what you do notable and, therefore, important. I think both these effects are to be desired, especially for the new and as yet uncertain writer, and so I recommend the exercise.

A diary, of course, takes its name from the fact of its being a *daily* record, but few people can really order their lives to make a daily entry possible, so many of the things we have that are called diaries are in fact journals. Unless you are in the midst of truly momentous events that actually do need to be recorded every single day (something like being the chief aide to Churchill during World War II) most likely you will only get to your diary or day book when you have spare time. I include such books here because in their spirit and effect there is no real difference between a diary and a journal. They can be kept strictly for yourself or perhaps for your children and in any case you expect to control who sees them, if anyone ever does. You are thus free in a way you cannot be when you know others will be looking in and making comments, judgments, and criticisms.

Occasionally, however, diaries do get published, and some journals have been kept with a view to their publication, so they are sort of a simple beginning into writing for publication, a form that is much looser and much more random than most writing. That is why I begin with them and why much can be learned from them.

Let us, at the outset, consider an example. This is from *Java Diary,* by Eliot Elisofon, with an Introductory Letter by Charles A. Lindbergh.

Friday, August 25, 8 A.M.

On board the *Harini.* The engine now starts. At least, it's fixed for the moment.

I checked and found out that although the boat is fairly new, the engine is from a 1952 Dodge truck. The *Harini* is twelve meters long, four meters wide, and can carry ten tons. So says Ong Tjinbun.

Ong is small and wears a jacket and trousers of jungle cloth and a khaki beret—for which he'll substitute any borrowed hat he can get. The lighthouseman had a sailor hat, so Ong wore that while the man was aboard. The day the survey teams were getting ready, Ong carried one of the rifles. This morning he carried a guitar (without playing it) that belongs to one of the men cutting trails for Dr. Schenkel. He's quite a character. He and his crew are paid about $25 a day, whether the *Harini* runs or not. The cheapest yacht I ever hired.

9:05. Reached Kerantijopong, but no fruit bats visible. We are cruising back and forth looking.

August 25, 3:30 P.M.

I'm back at the tower now, writing again. I'm becoming more and more interested in this diary. I know it will mean something to my daughters, Elin and Jill, and possibly be interesting to others too. Perhaps only the fact that I have no one to talk to prompts this effort. If so, so be it.

I spent yesterday afternoon in the blind but I didn't record what happened. I'm sorry now, for trying to write about it today isn't the same as writing about it while it's going on.

On my way back to the tower I tasted one of the petals. I thought it would be very sweet, since monkeys, peacocks, and now hornbills eat the yellow flowers. But I found it bitter.

What is to be learned from this? In the first place it is pretty obvious that the author is not a writer. His narrative is disjointed, lacks form or coherence, and is without grace. He is, in fact, not a writer at all but a famous *Life* photographer, and the reason the book was published was because he went to a very exotic place to photograph flora and fauna that hadn't been well shown before, if they have been seen at all. The diary is just an excuse for a text. Every publisher knows that books of pictures, no matter how lovely, must have a text. The human eye takes in a picture all at once, in a sort of gestalt, and thus books that have nothing but pictures in them seem to have almost no content—or the content is so quickly apprehended that it seems to have no substance. For this reason every picture book needs text on almost every page to stop the eye and convince the reader that the book has indeed got some substance or else people will not take the book seriously enough to make it seem worth paying the high price that every picture book must command. This is the *National Geographic* lesson in publishing. No one is expected to read the articles—and almost no one does—but the articles have to be there. It has been found over and over again that *National Geographic* readers look at the pictures, read the captions, and then keep the magazine thinking that they will get around to the text when they have time later. That is why everybody keeps *National Geographic* but never actually reads it. They keep it the way people keep the complete works of Trollope—they feel that if it is there they *have* it and that is almost as good as actually reading it, and that if it is *there,* they can get around to it anytime. And so it is with Elisofon. His publisher had to have a text to go with Elisofon's pictures, so he used what was at hand, Elisofon's journal—although it certainly was not up to the usual level of published work, because when he wrote he did not expect anyone to read it.

In this case, Elisofon is, in fact, so self-depreciating that it shows that he does not consider himself a writer. In any case, the book was not a commercial success, and perhaps the weakness in the text may have been part of the reason.

For a writer hoping to be published this book has another lesson, which is that a lot of things get published for reasons that have nothing to do with the skill of the author, as we see here and will see any number of times later on in this book. What that means is that writing for publication does not always mean writing well, but being involved with a project that needs something written, no matter how ineptly. It is not the way I would wish readers of this book to prepare themselves for publication—it is only an observation upon getting published. The truth is that a lot of writers get published who write no better than Elisofon or than you do right now. What that means is that there is no reason for you not to aspire to do better and to bring your writing up to a publishable level by a little hard work.

It may be a bit of a digression at this point, perhaps, but I think it is worth noting here that many well-known writers have found it useful not to keep a diary, but to keep a sort of notebook. Somerset Maugham did so all his life, putting down random bits of things that interested him, sketches, short characterizations, ideas, anything he thought worth keeping. He had a long and highly successful career as a writer, and although his books are not read so much now and his plays are largely forgotten, nonetheless his *Of Human Bondage* remains a classic, and his career remains a lesson in solid professionalism. His notebooks were published with the title *A Writer's Notebook* and they can be read by any aspiring writer who wants to see how his mind worked. Here is an extract:

The missionary. He was a tall thin man, with long limbs loosely jointed, hollow cheeks and high cheek-bones; his fine large dark eyes were deep in their sockets, and he had full sensual lips; he wore his hair rather long. He had a cadaverous look, and a look of suppressed fire. His hands were large, rather finely shaped, with long fingers, and his naturally pale skin was deeply burned by the Pacific sun.

Mrs. W., his wife, was a little woman with her hair very elaborately done, with prominent blue eyes behind gold-rimmed *pince-nez;* her face was long, like a sheep's, but she gave no impression of foolishness, rather of extreme alertness. She had the quick movements of a bird. The most noticeable thing about her was her voice, high, metallic and without inflection; it fell on the ear with a hard monotony, irritating the nerves like the clamour of a pneumatic drill. She was dressed in black, and wore round her neck a thin gold chain from which hung a small cross. She was a New Englander. Mrs. W. told me that her husband was a medical missionary, and as his district (the Gilberts) consisted of widely separated islands, he frequently had to go long distances by canoe. The sea was often rough and his journeys were not without danger. During his absence she remained at their headquarters and managed the mission. She spoke of the depravity of the natives in a voice nothing could hush, but with a vehement, unctuous horror; she described their marriage customs as obscene beyond description. She said that when first they went to the Gilberts it was impossible to find a single 'good' girl in any of the villages. She was very bitter about the dancing.

Miss Thompson. Plump, pretty in a course fashion, perhaps not more than twenty-seven: she wore a white dress and a large white hat, and long white boots from which her calves, in white cotton stockings, bulged. She had left Iweldi after the raid and was on her way to Apia, where she hoped to get a job in the bar of a hotel. She was brought to the house by the quartermaster, a little, very wrinkled man, indescribably dirty.

The lodging house. It is a two-storey frame house with verandas on both floors, and it [is] about five minutes' walk from the dock, on the Broad Road, and faces the sea. Below is a store in which are sold canned goods, pork and beans, beef, hamburger steak, canned asparagus, peaches and apricots; and cotton goods, lava-lavas, hats, rain-coats and such like. The owner is a half-caste with a native wife surrounded by little brown children. The rooms are almost bare of furniture, a poor iron bed with a ragged mosquito-curtain, a rickety chair and a washstand. The rain rattles down on the corrugated iron roof. No meals are provided.

On these notes I constructed a story called "Rain."

Out of nothing more solid than this came what was perhaps his most famous short story—"Rain." The lesson is that *anything* you keep, if it interests you, may prove to be valuable.

Now let us turn to a true diary, and this example I label *good.*

Saturday, 1 May, 1943

Dear Kitty,

If I just think of how we live here, I usually come to the conclusion that it is a paradise compared with how other

Jews who are not in hiding must be living. Even so, later on, when everything is normal again, I shall be amazed to think that we, who were so spick and span at home, should have sunk to such a low level. By this I mean that our manners have declined. For instance, ever since we have been here, we have had one oilcloth on our table which, owing to so much use, is not one of the cleanest. Admittedly I often try to clean it with a dirty dishcloth, which is more hole than cloth. The table doesn't do us much credit either, in spite of hard scrubbing. The Van Daans have been sleeping on the same flannelette sheet the whole winter; one can't wash it here because the soap powder we get on the ration isn't sufficient, and besides it's not good enough. Daddy goes about in frayed trousers and his tie is beginning to show signs of wear too. Mummy's corsets have split today and are too old to be repaired, while Margot goes about in a brassiere two sizes too small for her.

Mummy and Margot have managed the whole winter with three vests between them, and mine are so small that they don't even reach my tummy.

Certainly, these are all things which can be overcome. Still, I sometimes realize with a shock: "How are we, now going about in worn-out things, from my pants down to Daddy's shaving brush, ever going to get back to our prewar standards?"

They were banging away so much last night that four times I gathered all my belongings together. Today I have packed a suitcase with the most necessary things for an escape. But Mummy quite rightly says: "Where will you escape to?" The whole of Holland is being punished for the strikes which have been going on in many parts of the country. Therefore a state of siege has been declared and everyone gets one butter coupon less. What naughty little children!

Yours, Anne

Tuesday, May 18, 1943

This is, of course, from *Anne Frank: The Diary of a Young Girl,* probably the most famous and touching diary to have come out of World War II. Published in over thirty countries in thirty-one languages and adapted for Broadway under the title of *The Diary of Anne Frank,* it has brought to life the horror of the holocaust. Anne and her whole family were hidden for over two years; finally betrayed to the Gestapo, they were sent to the concentration camps where everyone but her father perished. It is the knowledge of her fate that makes her artless, hopeful, and confused responses to her life and growth so affecting.

Written when she was fourteen years old, these letters to her imaginary friend, Kitty, include small domestic matters that seemed so important to a family entirely confined in a secret attic as well as glimpses of how the great war raging all around them impinged upon their daily lives. It is precisely because we know that this diary was entirely private when it was written and that the author suffered an appalling death soon after the last entry in it that it carries such weight. Ernest Schnabel, who wrote a book about her that was published in 1958, says, "Her voice was preserved out of the millions that were silenced, this voice no louder than a child's whisper. . . . It has outlasted the shouts of the murderers and has soared above the voices of time." And he is right.

Given the natural albeit raw talent she evinces in her diary, Anne Frank probably could have become a very good writer had she lived. It is nonetheless true that if Anne Frank had survived and presented this diary to a publisher after the war when she had become a solid bourgeois housewife with several children around her skirts, the publisher would in all likelihood have thought it not worth publishing. If all her fears had been for nothing and all the family's hardships in the secret attic but the price they paid for their survival, then her wartime diary of how she suffered her growing pains in hiding would have been of interest merely to her children. She would have been in the same position as the French aristocrat who, when asked what he did during the French Revolution, replied, "I survived."

After something as special as Anne Frank's writings, we need to consider diaries and journals of a much more familiar kind. All these that follow I would put in the category of *better,* for they all have become more or less famous, and for good reason.

Of the several familiar sorts of diaries, the most obvious and probably one of the most useful is that written by a great person in the midst of great events. Our own founding fathers were all people who were aware of the momentous nature of what they were doing. The diaries of George Washington, John Adams, and Gouverneur Morris are all historical documents of the first importance, as their authors knew they would be even as they kept them. There is no substitute for writing down one's impressions of an event or a debate as soon as possible—that very day if one can— since the passage of even a day or two can dull the memory or shift the emphasis. A faithfully kept diary, which is probably as authentic an account of events as we are likely to get, is the raw material of history. Those who know they are making history or are seeing others make it tend to keep diaries, and those who write history later are grateful to them for it.

Wars are, of course, one of the most obvious historical events and every war has its share of diarists who recorded their part in the conflict. The American Civil War and World War II both brought out innumerable accounts, some of them appearing only much later. In 1987, for example, *Berlin Diaries, 1940–1945,* by Marie Vassiltchikov, was published. A White Russian princess who had grown up in Germany, she had seen the destruction of Berlin at firsthand. Her vantage point as an outsider in Germany let her see what Germans themselves were blind to, and her shrewd judgments were later validated by events. Like many valuable diaries, she gives a good picture of everyday life, the kind of mundane details of people's existence that one does not get from newspapers and official accounts and thus gives us insight into things that are usually not recorded at all.

For those eras before the explosion of public-information, diaries have served as one of our best glimpses into the social life of the times. For instance, in what was published as *The Diary of Philip Hone, 1828–1851,* that former mayor of New York City recorded the events he considered worth remembering. The following extracts are taken from his entries for 1839:

Thursday, Jan. 3.—The new Governor seems from the following article in the paper to excite some interest in Albany. "The number of visitors at the Governor's house to-day was not an assemblage, but a crowd, a jam, a multitude. The Governor had five tables tastefully arranged and abundantly provided with hams, cold turkeys, round of beef, and all other eatables and drinkables. There was a most eager desire to see the new chief magistrate, and when the crowd outside had increased to an uncountable multitude, the Governor appeared at one of the windows, and told them he was sorry his home could not contain all his friends. He hoped to meet them all hereafter, severally. His little speech was well received, and the thousands went away in good humor."

Monday, Jan. 7.—*Steamer Royal William.* The ability of the steam packets to make a westerly winter passage from Europe is now tested. The *Royal William* arrived here yesterday, having sailed from Liverpool the 15th of December.

The Club dined at Mr. Russell's, Messrs. Duer and Colt absent. We had among the supernumeraries Mr. Webster, who is here on his way to Washington. He was in exuberant spirits, and more agreeable than I have seen him on any former occasion. We sat until 11 o'clock and broke up after a grand chorus of "Auld Lang Syne."

Thursday, Jan. 17.—*Center Market.* A new market has been erected fronting on Center Street and extending from Spring to Broome Street. It is a handsome edifice, of brick closed in with doors and windows, much the finest market in the city, and promises to be a great accommodation to us uptown people. There was a great ball in the upper saloons of the market this evening, at which it is said one thousand persons sat down to dinner.

Thursday, Jan. 24.—*Investigating Committee.* One of the hardest fights the two political parties in Congress have ever had has just terminated in favor of the Whigs by a small majority. It arose on the appointment of a committee to investigate the causes of the late defalcations here and elsewhere. The Whigs proposed that instead of leaving the appointments to the Speaker, who would of course appoint a majority of birds of his own feather, and thereby stifle all inquiry which might tend to inculpate their own party, and expose the misdeeds of the administration, the selection should be made by ballot. This, of course, so obviously fair if the suspected parties are innocent and wish to have it proved, was violently opposed by Cambreleng and the rest of the Loco-focos, who threw every obstacle in the way of a fair investigation. But it was adopted. It was some time before three Van Buren men could be found to accept the appointment.

Monday, Jan. 28.—I heard a capital sermon yesterday morning in Trinity Church from Prof. McVickar of Columbia College. He does not often treat us; but when he does, it is a treat indeed. He comes with a sermon well prepared, logical, learned, of the purest English, and a style surpassingly beautiful.

I remember John McVickar a child in his father's house, at which time I, a boy not much older than himself, was frequently a visitor and sometimes an intimate of the family. He then stuttered in the most painful manner. He was a deep student, and seemed at that early age to be preparing for a profession in which that impediment in speaking would prove a fatal obstacle; so he patiently and laboriously went to work on the

Demosthenian plan, and recited and harangued daily, his mouth filled with pebbles, until he conquered in a great measure his infirmity.

The example demonstrates the width of Hone's interests and the varied nature of the events of his life that seemed worth recording. He is not a very good writer, but he has a sharp eye for character and although he is very judgmental one feels that his is a fair picture of the men he describes. Between the diaries of Hone and those of the much more famous George Templeton Strong, whose great four-volume journal covers the years 1835–1875, we have a lively and immediate sense of life in New York City for quite a stretch. Although both men are old-school conservatives, without them we would have much less understanding of the social life and the cares of the ordinary folk of the time. Reading them, we feel that these diaries were not meant to be kept private. What readers they may have had in mind is never stated, but one assumes that at the least they were keeping their diaries for family and friends, if not for the historical record itself.

Less instructive to the beginning writer, but more important historically, are journals kept on voyages of exploration and discovery. Some of them have quite rightly become very famous and will remain so. Among the multitude of similar daybooks, the journal of Christopher Columbus, Lewis and Clark's journals, and *The Voyage of the Beagle* by Charles Darwin are of the first historical and scientific importance. My favorite journalist is the ornithological artist John James Audubon. Here is a sample from *Audubon, by Himself*:

> After six weeks the river fell swiftly. A channel began to appear amid the ice. All was bustle as we prepared to depart for Cape Girardeau. We and the Indians parted like brethren. Navigation was most dangerous, as we propelled the boat against the ice with long poles, or against the bottom wherever we could

touch it. With the ice higher than our heads our progress was extremely slow. Fortune was with us, and we reached the Cape.

The little village contained nothing remarkable or interesting except the father of our patroon, an original indeed, and a representative of a class of men fast disappearing from the earth. His portrait is so striking and well worth preserving that I shall try to draw it for you:

Imagine a man not more than four feet six, thin in proportion, looking as if just shot out of a pop-gun. His nose formed, decidedly, the most prominent feature of his spare, meager countenance. It was a true *nez à la Grand Frederic*—a tremendous promontory fully three inches in length—hooked like a Hawk's beak and garnished with eyes like an Eagle's. His hair was plastered down close to his head with a quantity of pomatum; it ended in a long *queue* rolled up in a dirty ribbon that hung down below his waist. The upper part of his dress was European, once rich but now woefully patched and dilapidated, with shreds of gold and silver lace here and there. The fashion of his waistcoat, as antique as that of his nose, had immense pocket flaps that covered more than half his tight buckskin trousers that were ornamented with big, iron knee-buckles, to support Indian hunting gaiters long past their prime. His moccasins, to complete his costume, were really of the most beautiful workmanship. Though these articles of dress, along with his stature and singular features, made him the most ludicrous caricature imaginable, his manners were courteous and polished. He said he had been Louisiana governor when it was a Spanish possession. Since his retirement to this little village he had come to be looked upon as a great General and was held in highest esteem.

We proceeded to Grand Tower, and round its immense rock against which the current crashed, without mishap. All night we heard the howling of Wolves from the hills of the Illinois shore. I thought them hunting Deer in packs, like dogs, but with more sagacity and cunning. They drive the game before them toward Wolves, posted in ambush, which overtake their prey.

It is well known that a cry brings the pack, somewhat in a way a hunter's bugle sounds the death note.

We arrived safely at Ste. Genevieve, an old French town—small and dirty. I far preferred the time I had spent in Tawapatee Bottom. I waited only for a thaw to return home. The ice broke at last. Bidding Rozier good-by, I whistled to my dog, crossed the Mississippi, and was on the road on foot and alone, bound for Shawanee Town. But I found the prairies covered with seas of water. My desire to rejoin my family made me oblivious to all else. My moccasins constantly slipped, so that wading became irksome. Nevertheless I made forty-five miles and swam the Muddy River that first day out, and saw only two cabins. Deer stood ankle-deep in water. Thousands of Buffalo skulls lay about, just appearing above the water.

I made straight for a curl of smoke that promised a good dinner. The boys of the house examined my handsome double-barreled gun while their mother and sister ground coffee, fired venison, and cooked eggs. The kind hostess was stirring at daybreak to get me a good breakfast and would take no recompense, so I gave each boy a horn of powder—a rare and valuable article to a squatter in those days. I left another forty-five miles behind me by nightfall, and camped that night with a party of Indians beside a canebrake. I awoke to find—to my surprise—that all the Indians had departed with their guns and left only two dogs to guard the camp from Wolves. I was now about forty miles from Shawanee. My dog knew very well that he was near home and seemed happy as I was. I met no one all day, and found no cabin on the road. At 4 o'clock I passed the first salt well. Half an hour later I was at the village inn, with friends who had come to purchase salt, forty-seven miles from home. The next day, to my great joy, brought me to my family, and to the end of this pleasant excursion.

Now I find this splendid. Audubon's obvious good humor, indefatigable curiosity, complete openness, and infectious zest for life seem to me irresistible. Look how the old man he describes comes to life, "looking as if just shot out of a pop-gun." Imagine a man who thinks nothing of walking forty-five miles a day in freezing weather, who carries nothing with him except his gun and his powder, and never loses his cheerfulness. A natural writer, he can only stand as a splendid lesson for us all and certainly one of the finest examples of the outlook of the explorer.

If one were to look for a writer completely at the other end of the spectrum from that represented by Audubon, nothing could offer a contrast more stark than that offered by a self-conscious literary writer such as Virginia Woolf. She is not to my taste, and so I won't quote from one of her books, but it should be noted that many people have found her diaries interesting, and she is something of a cult figure. Even more firmly established as a cult figure is Anaïs Nin. As with other cults, it is not always easy for the outsider to see the immense attraction it offers. I remember talking to her London publisher some years ago as he was bringing out yet another volume of her diaries. He had no idea who read them as he himself had no interest in doing so, but he wearily persisted in each volume and someone out there bought them. He couldn't imagine why, and I don't know either, but literary tastes are as varied as the whole range of people who write, so it is not for a mere publisher to discourage people who want to read something. The lesson, I think, is that for a writer to absolutely dedicate herself to being a literary figure success comes from total absorption in playing that role. Being a writer is what they *are* and all other aspects of their lives and activities are strictly secondary. It is, perhaps, this complete wrapping of oneself into a blanket called being a writer that I find suffocating but which fascinates a special but considerable following.

For the student of literature and of writing in general, the diaries of important authors like Franz Kafka and Thomas Mann can obviously be very helpful in understanding how great works came to be and what kind of person wrote them.

I was interested to know, for example, that Mann seemed to think that he had done a day's work if he completed a page or a page and a half. Could I do as much? Of course. Could you? Why not? You won't end up with *The Magic Mountain*, but your friends may think what you've done is great.

The range, then, of all kinds of diaries that we will call *better* is very wide indeed. We read diaries of note less often for purely literary reasons than for the more practical purpose of getting interesting or important raw information firsthand.

When we come to consider what we would take to be the *best* example of a diary, there seems little doubt that anyone at all familiar with English literature would agree that no diary is better written or more important than that of Samuel Pepys.

Samuel Pepys lived in seventeenth-century London during an extraordinary time, a turbulent, wide-open, licentious, and brawling time, an era of sudden disaster, change, and great fortunes made and suddenly lost. Pepys lived through the Dutch War in a position we would now call Secretary of the Navy, stayed in London through the great plague, witnessed the Great Fire, knew everybody of interest or power, and applied his curiosity and energy to whatever came across his path. He was in every respect a man of parts and his diary, vivid, pulsing with life, frank, and completely without guile is one of the great documents of an age that now seems somehow both familiar but also utterly remote. Here, chosen almost at random, are a few samples from *Everybody's Pepys: The Diary of Samuel Pepys, 1660–1669:*

> *4th.* To my office, and there all the morning. At noon to dinner to my Lord Belasses, where he told us a very handsome passage of the King's sending him his message about holding out the town of Newarke, of which he was then governor for the King. This message he sent in a slugg-bullet, being writ in cypher, and

wrapped up in lead and swallowed. So the messenger come to my Lord and told him he had a message from the King but it was yet in his belly; so they did give him some physique, and out it come. This was a month before the King's flying to the Scotts; and therein he told him that at such a day, being the 3d or 6th of May, he should hear of his being come to the Scotts; and at the just day he did come to the Scotts. He told us another odd passage: how the King having newly put out Prince Rupert of his generalship, upon some miscarriage at Bristoll, the great officers of the King's army mutinyed, and come in that manner with swords drawn into the market-place of the towne where the King was; which the King hereing, says, "I must to horse." And there himself personally, when every body expected they should have been opposed, the King come, and cried to the head of the mutineers, which was Prince Rupert, "Nephew, I command you to be gone." So the Prince, in all his fury and discontent withdrew, and his company scattered; which they say was the greatest piece of mutiny in the world.

9th. Sir William Petty tells me that Mr. Barlow is dead; for which, God knows my heart, I could be as sorry as is possible for one to be for a stranger, by whose death he gets £100 per annum, he being a worthy, honest man; but after having considered that when I come to consider the providence of God by this means unexpectedly to give me £100 a year more in my estate, I have cause to bless God, and do it from the bottom of my heart.

5th. (Lord's Day.) Made a visit to Mr. Evelyn, who among other things showed me most excellent painting in little, in distemper, Indian incke, water colours, graveing; and above all, the whole secret of mezzo-tinto and the manner of it, which is very pretty, and good things done with it. He read to me very much also of his discourse he hath been many years and now is about, about Guardenage, which will be a most noble and pleasant piece. He read me part of a play or two of his making, very good, but not as he conceits them, I think, to be. He showed me his Hortus Hyemalis; leaves laid up in a book of several plants kept dry, which preserve colour, however, and look very finely, better than any Herball. In fine, a most excellent person he is, and must be allowed a little for a little conceitedness; but he may well be so, being a man so much above others. He read me, though with too much gusto, some little poems of his own, that were not transcendent, yet one or two very pretty epigrams; among others, of a lady looking in at a grate, and being pecked at by an eagle that was there.

Reading Pepys is like eating popcorn and yet his diary stands as a major document of its age, due partly to the paucity of other records of the daily life of the times but also to the vividness with which we can conjure up that life after having read it. The mad race for money, the hectic daily round of the townspeople, the openness of appetite, and the hazardous immediacy of life all are abundantly evident and all conveyed without any notion on Pepys's part that this is what he is showing. He just tells us what he did and saw, but his energy, curiosity, and utter candor bring it to life. There is no other diary like it.

What, then, is to be learned from thinking about or keeping a journal? Writing was invented as an *aide memoire,* literally a mnemonic device, a system of keeping the King's records of the grain in his storehouse. Ancient writing consists of lists of things, tax rolls, inventories—what we would now think of as bookkeeping. It proved to be a powerful way to aid the fallible human memory and only after it was well established in its record-keeping function did writing start to be used in more personal ways. Diaries and journals fulfill this primitive function to this day, nonetheless powerful for being an ancient usage. Anne Lister's diaries have only now come to light. An heiress who lived in West Yorkshire, she kept a diary from 1791 to 1840 because she wanted to have "a private memorial that I may hereafter read, perhaps with a smile, when Time has frozen up the channel of those sentiments which flow so freshly now." Her candor seems the equal of James Boswell, Rousseau, or, of course, Pepys and thus what she says is valuable. But her aim, like that of most diarists, was only the simple one of remembering.

For the beginning writer, a diary is good exercise, a safe way to practice without exposing what you do to others' eyes and a way of remembering as effective now as it ever was. Try it, you might like it. Art will come later.

MEMOIRS

EVERYONE HAS HAD AN UPBRINGING. Everyone has a memory. Things happened to you that happened to no one else. What you have done and seen can only be shared if you write down your recollection of things you have known. Your life *is*, in a sense, your memory. To fix it and to keep it, you write your memories down.

When it comes to learning writing I always ask my students to start with a memoir. It is the easiest and most natural form for the beginner to take up, and not only because you don't need to do any research to do it. It is important because it reminds you of your own unique position in the universe, the fleeting nature of memory, and how strongly it is possible to feel about events and people that you are surprised that you can recall. Memoirs are for family and for children and for the record book. Memoirs are for getting it straight and for putting what you have done in perspective. While some may think that it is self-centered and presumptuous to write them, I think that attitude is nonsense. If you need justification, merely think of writing memoirs as a literary exercise that I have recommended, as would anyone hoping to teach you how to write better.

To begin with, take a single episode and try and bring it back to life. Don't tell it; show it. That is the oldest and simplest of all advice to writers, and every writing book will say the same thing, but it is usually not that easy for the as-yet-unpracticed to do. People have a tendency to hold back from emotion and color, to just tell things in a flat and distant fashion.

A student will write, "When I was little we used to get taken to the beach by my uncle and all the kids had a lot of fun." Told that this isn't really very satisfactory and that it doesn't convey any flavor, the student may try again and come up with something more like this: "When I was about eight or nine, my uncle got a panel truck to make deliveries for the grocery store he ran, and on Saturdays he didn't need to use it for the store, so he could take all us kids to the beach in it. We didn't have a car in those days, and the beach was a long way off, so without the truck we couldn't have gotten there. On a summer Saturday we'd all pile in the back of it, eight or nine of us, and start off. The panel truck didn't have any windows in the back, so we couldn't see out and there weren't any seats either, so we sat on empty fruit boxes in the back, and they slid all around as we bumped on down the road. To keep the others from pinching and biting Alfredo, who was the littlest, and my youngest brother, Mama would turn around in the seat up front and lead us all in singing Italian songs that she remembered from Naples. That's how I learned all Mama's songs when I was little. Somehow it never seemed to be a long time until we got to the beach."

Clearly an improvement, this paragraph still could use some color and possibly the hint of a plot, but it is moving in the right direction.

One thing that the novice writer should always remember is that telling too much is far better than not telling enough. If you adopt a professional attitude from the beginning, you will know that not everything you do will be as effective as everything else, and thus cutting what you write can often improve the effect of the whole. Any good editor can cut a manuscript to make it tighter, but no editor can add what is missing. Thus, if a new writer is to make a mistake, it should be in the way of doing too much. Thomas Wolfe, of course, is the famous American writer who produced much too much, writing compulsively and constantly and piling up millions of words and then more millions until there were trunks full of the stuff and no one could seem to make sense of it all, least of all Wolfe himself. While this picture is somewhat exaggerated, there is much truth in it. But would we rather have had too much of him or too little? I think too much is always better, for then the best can be dug out and the rest left to scholars and the family. Would Wolfe be famous now if he had written a few perfect short stories and three tightly drawn novels? One wonders. Having been an editor myself, I am perhaps too quick to take the editorial point of view, but any writer can act as his own editor, and, indeed, should. For a beginning writer, it is certainly true that there is no such thing as too much. A lot of practice is essential.

Thus my advice is to start with a memoir. Write about something quite specific and precise. The best memoirs are of some characteristic event, such as a day in the country, and focus on just a few people, showing what they are like and how they think and speak. It may help some writers to think in cinematic terms—that is, in pictures—and describe events as a sort of series of pictures. Other writers like to deal with the intricacies of relationships, showing how different people react to each other: Papa being kind and indulgent, or Papa being overbearing with his cousin, or Papa in an uneasy truce with Mama. It doesn't matter what you choose as long as you *show* it.

Let's say that the family is preparing for a day in the country, but Papa can't find the baseball and bat. How does Mama react? The beginning writer will tell us that the kids all thought it was very funny that Papa couldn't find the bat, but the more experienced writer will show us a little drama in action and bring it alive.

We are now ready for our first example of memoir, a

passage from *Young in New York* by Nathalie Dana. This charming extract we label *good:*

I was born into a society which was sure that it had found the answers. Our life was contained within the limits of my father's Episcopal parish in the Lenox Hill Section of New York, but it formed a pattern repeated again and again in Victorian America. We lived by a code, based on religion, which told us what was right and what was wrong; we felt secure financially; and except for occasional trips, we stayed in the same place. Life seemed settled once and for all, and we did not expect it to change.

There was no inheritance tax and no income tax in those days. A man could thriftily build up a fortune which would guarantee lifelong security to his children, and conscientious men systematically saved with this end in view. Once when I was enjoying the attentions of a man my father disliked he told me that I did not have to marry as I could always count on an income of $5,000 a year which then would maintain me in comfort.

The uneven distribution of wealth was not a matter of concern. It seemed a pity that there were so many poor people, but as this was a part of "God's own plan," what could one do but send them turkeys at Thanksgiving and blankets at Christmas and see that they did not starve when they were sick? When Horace Mann led a crusade urging that the education of children should become a public responsibility he was opposed on the ground that his proposal invaded the field of individual initiative and furnished education to those "who were better without it."

In the age of walking and horseback riding the pace was slow. Men walked to their offices even when they were several miles away, and only occasionally did women take the long trip to the shops in a horsecar. Most activities were local and life was leisurely.

Into these secure surroundings subdued happiness came as the first streaks of dawn appeared on a hot June morning in

1878. At that moment my mother gave birth to a daughter. The delivery took place in her bed of dark carved oak, in the customary Victorian way, under a sheet. Now she had what she had longed for, two sons and two daughters, and her joy was shared by the whole family. The baby's unfashionable red hair was overlooked.

The day was Whitsunday, and to an Episcopalian household this was important. Whitsunday was the festival of the Church which celebrated the descent of the Holy Spirit to the disciples in tongues of fire and a rushing, mighty wind; a birth on this day was a special sign of God's grace. Life had now been given to compensate for the life which had been taken on Easter Day six weeks before, when the baby's grandfather, Nathan Smith, had died. Easter was the best day to leave the world, and now the baby came on a special day. It was mysterious, like a sign from heaven. The rejoicing was great.

There are several things to notice here. The first of them is that Mrs. Dana is in fact that rare example of a pure amateur writer. She had no training or special practice as a writer before she decided to write her memoirs. She had an unremarkable life in many ways, but she always lived without money worries and circulated among the best of society. Her education had been good at a time when girls were seldom given much education at all. Her life had been secure, happy, and satisfying, and her memoir had not the slightest hint of regret or doubt.

When I first read this it was in the early 1950s, and although Mrs. Dana was elderly by then, a lot of older ladies had lived lives not markedly dissimilar to hers. Since the older editors at Doubleday had heard a lot about the Victorian period from their parents, these memoirs seemed pretty routine to them, many of whom had parents who were older than Mrs. Dana then was. The younger editors, however, thought this was a charming, unaffected, revelation of what New York had been like long before they knew it, and we wanted to publish it. At the time, though, we couldn't get enough support from our elders and so the book was turned down. After only ten years, though, opinion changed in the Doubleday editorial department; someone remembered the manuscript, asked for it back, and persuaded a reluctant department to publish it. Much to the surprise of the older group, the book proved to be a considerable success and went through several editions. The charm of its openness and innocence and the picture it gave of a secure but still dynamic society attracted many for whom Mrs. Dana's style of life was a surprise.

In case any modern reader should miss the clues to her naïveté about writing and life that Mrs. Dana strews about, it should be remembered that she leaves a few important things out. In the first place, she neither tells us nor seems to know that her father, as the rector of St. James Church, stood very high up in the ranks of the Episcopal Church. St. James, then and now, was the fashionable uptown church that the rich and powerful attended. The rector there would stand second only to the rector of Trinity Church, at the end of Wall Street, in the church hierarchy, and above *him* there was only a bishop. Thus her father was no mere parish priest with a humble and honest flock—quite the contrary, he presided over the church to which the rich who were building their mansions along Fifth Avenue went every Sunday. It would be to one of those great houses stuffed with servants that he would go for sherry after Sunday service. Both he and his daughter took this entirely for granted.

Further, Mrs. Dana does not note, although we should, that around 1900, her guaranteed income of $5,000 a year meant that she was rich. When Mrs. Dana was twenty, she perhaps thought that such a sum would make her "comfortable," but we should know that today's equivalent would be about $100,000.

Aside from the facts she presents in her account, what does her writing tell us? It stands as an example of how an open, unaffected, and untutored writer can catch and keep our attention with her subject rather than her style. We want to know how this little girl lived and to glimpse her family and the larger society in which they lived. That she is a natural writer with an unforced and familiar style makes it all the more appealing. Because she was interested in what went on around her and didn't care to describe her personal development, she is an open-eyed reporter of her times. Her own complete lack of *angst* tells us almost as much as her observations of great houses being built along Fifth Avenue as she walks to school. Thus her unaffectedness, which no professional writer could imitate successfully, is central not only to her presentation but to our response to it. Her ingenuousness makes her account valuable and should help to inspire other amateur writers to attempt to write their own memoirs.

Something else should be noted here as well. Not a few successful writers have started on their careers when they read something and thought to themselves, "Why, I could do that." They then tried to imitate a book they had read and found that they could do it perfectly well. In fact, that is a good exercise for any aspiring writer. Several authors that I know who write formulaic Western, Romance, or mystery books started that way. Often, having gained self-confidence from doing something recognized and commercial, they then go on to more "literary" and original work. But for any aspiring writer it is a good exercise to read things and ask yourself—could I do that? Here is Mrs. Dana, with little formal education and no previous experience in writing, turning out a charming memoir. If she can do it, why can't you? Your answer should be, well, there really isn't any good reason why I can't. If that's the case, then that should be enough to start you writing a memoir.

At this point we consider another *good* example, this from *The Autobiography of Lincoln Steffens:*

> Early in the morning of April 6, 1866, in a small house "over in the Mission" of San Francisco, California, I was born—a remarkable child. This upon the authority of my mother, a

remarkable woman, who used to prove her prophetic judgment to all listeners till I was old enough to make my own demonstration.

Even then, though I was there to frown her down, she was ever ready to bring forth her evidence, which opened with the earthquake of 1868. When that shock shook most San Franciscans out of their houses into the streets, she ran upstairs to me and found me pitched out of bed upon the floor but otherwise unmoved. As she said with swimming eyes, I was "not killed, not hurt, and, of course, not crying; I was smiling, as always, good as gold."

My own interpretation of this performance is that it was an exhibit less of goodness than of wisdom. I knew that my mother would not abandon me though the world rocked and the streets yawned. Nor is that remarkable. Every well-born baby is sure he can trust his mother. What strikes me as exceptional and promising in it is that I had already some sense of values; I could take such natural events as earthquakes all in my stride. That, I think, is why I smiled then; that is why I smile now; and that may be why my story is of a happy life—happier and happier. Looking back over it now for review, it seems to me that each chapter of my adventures is happier than the preceding chapters right down to this, the last one: age, which, as it comes, comes a-laughing, the best of all. I have a baby boy of my own now; my first—a remarkable child, who—when he tumbles out of bed—laughs; as good as gold.

I was well-born. My mother, Elizabeth Louisa Symes, was an English girl who came from New York via the Isthmus of Panama to San Francisco in the sixties to get married. It was rumored about the east that the gold rush of '49 had filled California with men oolf aelccted, venturesome, strong young fellows who were finding there gold, silver, and everything else that they sought, excepting only wives. There was a shortage of women of the marriageable sort. My mother had highly developed the woman's gift of straight-seeing, practical intelligence which makes for direct action. She not only knew that she, like all girls, wanted a husband; she acknowledged it to herself and took steps to find one. There was no chance for her in the crowded east; competition was too sharp for the daughters of a poor family like hers. She would go west. A seamstress, she could always earn a living there or anywhere. She took one of her sisters, Emma, and they went to the easiest man-market in the world at that time, and there, in San Francisco, they promptly married two young men chums whom they met at their first boarding-house. They paired off, and each married the other's beau; otherwise it turned out just as these two wise maidens had planned. This on the authority of my father, who loved and laughed to tell it thus when my mother was there to hear; it annoyed and pleased her so. She was an amiable, teasable wife. He was a teasing, jesting father with a working theory that a fact is a joke.

My father was one of the sixteen or seventeen children of a pioneer farmer of eastern Canada, who drove west with his wife in a wagon to Illinois, where he bought, cleared, and worked his piece of wilderness, raised his big herd of tall boys and strong girls, and, finally, died in 1881, eighty-one years of age. He was a character, this grandfather of mine. I saw him once. My mother took me and my sister to visit him when we were very small, and I remember how, bent with age and brooking, he gradually looked up, saw us, said "Humph," and went back into himself for his silence. He came to life only one other time for me. I was looking at a duster made of horsehairs that was stuck in a knot-hole on a board fence. It looked just like a horse's tail, and I was peering through a crack to see the horse. My grandfather, watching me, said, "The horse was cut off the tail." I wondered, but he did not laugh, so I believed him.

Steffens was one of the most important and lastingly influential journalists of his time—the famous muckraker whose exposés of corruption in government led, at least in part, to a whole new public attitude about how governments should be run in this country. It is remarkable that this passage, written when he was sixty-three or sixty-four, should sound so self-conscious: it is somewhat awkward, hesitant, and not a little stilted—all qualities that characterize an amateur writer. Perhaps the reason lies in Steffens's being self-conscious about writing about himself when he has spent a lifetime looking out and fixing his interest on what is going on around him. Certainly his reports of corruption as he saw it in action show no such hesitancy. Nevertheless, his *Autobiography* remains an important American book because of its truthful and uncompromising picture of what the country was like as he was reporting on it.

Yet even at its best his writing, *as writing,* is never more than rough and ready. He merely adheres to the style of the times, which was a bit more self-conscious than we are used to now. Here, for example, is his summing up of the defeat of Tammany in New York: "After Schmittberger's 'squeal,' other officers 'laid down' too. Byrnes resigned; other 'higher-ups' confessed; and the defeat of Tammany was assured."

That he should feel the need to put the slang words in quotation marks tells us that he knows that they are slang words and that, we, his readers, being delicate, will object to slang and only forgive his use of it if he shows us that he, too, knows they are slang. Well, it all seems a bit quaint today. In 1931, perhaps it was his publisher's editors who insisted on the quotation marks around those expressions, but his acceptance of such usage shows a concern for the genteel that even then seems almost odd. Still, anyone who reads his book today will find that most of it is brisk and completely straightforward reporting, enlivened by a good deal of dialogue that seems true-to-life.

The point of this is to notice that Steffens will never be remembered for *how* he wrote, but for *what* he wrote. Students of journalism will read him not to learn how to write but to see how a master got at the facts, and how his very lack of moral fervor made what he said believable. He keeps his distance from his subjects, as a good journalist should, and perhaps that is why, when it came to talking about himself, he suddenly got red-faced.

Now here is another example of a memoir that we label *good*. It is from *Five Boyhoods*.

When I was seven or eight or some such age, I was given a book called *The Real Diary of a Real Boy*. It was an account kept by a New England boy, Henry A. Shute, in the 1860's and rediscovered by him many years later. The diary so amused the grown Mr. Shute that he had it published, thinking that other readers might enjoy it. In my case he was right. The diary not only amused but fascinated me, for it recorded all the activities that I thought a real boy ought to be pursuing—and I was not.

I was an unreal American boy, or at least I had an unreal boyhood, innocent and sheltered. It was concentrated in the 1930's, and when that decade ended and I went off to college and the Army, boyhoods of this kind ended, too. War and taxes made them obsolete, and today not many boys grow up as isolated as I was. Probably this is just as well.

I grew up in the Town of Great Neck, on the north shore of Long Island, nineteen miles from New York. It was nowhere near as posh as the villages farther out on that gilded coast, like Locust Valley and Oyster Bay, but it did have a prosperous Republican look. We lived almost at the end of the neck, in an area called Kings Point, four miles from the railroad station and two from the town itself. The town was small and drowsy then, and the road to our house curved past many open fields, several woods, and a large pond. Other houses were scattered at fairly wide intervals along the way.

My parents built our large white shingle house in 1920, two years before I was born, when not many other families lived in that remote section, choosing a three-acre site which I always felt must be one of the most beautiful locations that any house could have. They built on a small hill overlooking the spot where Manhasset Bay widens to join Long Island Sound. A view across water is therefore one of my first memories. I could look miles up the Sound to a far-off land which I was told was Connecticut, and I soon fixed in my mind, with the help of binoculars, the pattern of houses in distant towns like New Rochelle and Port Washington.

Boats were my view. I watched them as other children watch cars and people going by. My favorites were the *Priscilla* and the *Commonwealth,* two aging white steamers of the Fall River Line. One of them passed every night at six on her voyage to sonorous Fall River, wherever that was, but surely an enchanted place if it could beckon these noble vessels with such unswerving regularity. Sometimes I could hear the music of their bands, and if I waited twenty minutes their waves would lap up on our beach, all power spent but a link nevertheless with the traffic of the seven seas. An hour later the night boat to Boston also passed. It was newer and sleeker than the *Priscilla* and the *Commonwealth,* but it lacked the jaded splendor of those old ladies, as well as a name to catch the imagination. The sister ships of this line were the *New York* and the *Boston,* and once I learned this dreary fact I no longer felt that they were worthy of a small boy's vigil on the sea wall.

That passage is by William Zinsser, whose book on writing I always recommend. Zinsser has been a professional writer for most of his adult life. The first work of his I read were his almost daily movie reviews for the old *Herald Tribune* in the 1950s. He could be very funny, and he was just about the only reviewer at that time who actually said what he thought about the movies he saw. His criticism had bite and style at a time when most movie reviewers did little, it seemed, but rewrite movie company publicity releases. He later went on to a career as editor, teacher, and writer and is a good example of the polished and confident practitioner who has made his living not only by being literate himself, but by being able to see the relative value of the literary efforts of others.

In the example above, he is, like Dana and Steffens, a bit self-conscious, but he still uses touches that neither an amateur nor a journalist would be likely to try. Consider "sonorous Fall River," or "the jaded splendor of those old ladies." These are sort of "writerly," if one can speak in those terms. They hardly show the inspiration of a major stylist, nor are they completely unself-conscious. They are instead the kind of thing a practiced writer uses as normal devices to convey his meaning—not so outlandish as to be misunderstood, but arresting enough to be original. The beginner can and should aspire to that level of writing.

Now we look at *Speak, Memory* by Vladimir Nabokov, a writer who is usually ranked among the *best:* .

> My father, let it be noted, had served his term of military training long before I was born, so I suppose he had that day put on the trappings of his old regiment as a festive joke. To a joke, then, I owe my first gleam of complete consciousness— which again has recapitulatory implications, since the first creatures on earth to become aware of time were also the first creatures to smile.
>
> It was the primordial cave (and not what Freudian mystics might suppose) that lay behind the games I played when I was four. A big cretonne-covered divan, white with black trefoils, in one of the drawing rooms at Vyra rises in my mind, like some massive product of a geological upheaval before the beginning of history. History begins (with the promise of fair Greece) not far from one end of this divan, where a large potted hydrangea shrub, with pale blue blossoms and some greenish ones, half concealed, in a corner of the room, the pedestal of a marble bust of Diana. On the wall against which the divan stands, another phase of history is marked by a gray engraving in an ebony frame—one of those Napoleonic-battle pictures in which the episodic and the allegoric are the real adversaries and where one sees, all grouped together on the same plane of vision, a wounded drummer, a dead horse, trophies, one soldier about to bayonet another, and the invulnerable emperor posing with his generals amid the frozen fray.
>
> With the help of some grown-up person, who would use first both hands and then a powerful leg, the divan would be moved

several inches away from the wall, so as to form a narrow passage which I would be further helped to roof snugly with the divan's bolsters and close up at the ends with a couple of its cushions. I then had the fantastic pleasure of creeping through that pitch-dark tunnel, where I lingered a little to listen to the singing in my ears—that lonesome vibration so familiar to small boys in dusty hiding places—and then, in a burst of delicious panic, on rapidly thudding hands and knees I would reach the tunnel's far end, push its cushion away, and be welcomed by a mesh of sunshine on the parquet under the canework of a Viennese chair and two gamesome flies settling by turns. A dreamier and more delicate sensation was provided by another cave game, and upon awakening in the early morning I made a tent of my bedclothes and let my imagination play in a thousand dim ways with shadowy snowslides of linen and with the faint light that seemed to penetrate my penumbral covert from some immense distance, where I fancied that strange, pale animals roamed in a landscape of lakes. The recollection of my crib, with its lateral nets of fluffy cotton cords, brings back, too, the pleasure of handling a certain beautiful, delightfully solid, garnet-dark crystal egg left over from some unremembered Easter; I used to chew a corner of the bedsheet until it was thoroughly soaked and then wrap the egg in it tightly, so as to admire and re-lick the warm, ruddy glitter of the snugly enveloped facets that came seeping through with a miraculous completeness of glow and color. But that was not yet the closest I got to feeding upon beauty.

Here is a modern master at work and it is a mistake to think that you will ever be able to write as he does. Nabokov, like Conrad and others, learned English only after he was deeply immersed in a foreign culture and language. He grew up Russian, later mastered—and mastered is the correct word—French, and only then learned and mastered English. Such depth of experience, feeling, and sensibility and such a range of words available for the expression of his fancies and delights are seldom in the equipment of a minor talent—but in the hands of a major one they can dazzle.

And dazzle he does. His pulse of emotion, his febrile delicacy of understanding, his switching from the greatest of cosmic questions to the smallest touch of color; his sense of the rush and thirst for life so immediate and compelling that we can only be borne along with him all confirm that we are helpless at the hands of genius. He knows he is a genius and assumes we know it too. He is then free to be as broad, as self-absorbed, as intimate, and as completely uninhibited as a balloonist rising silently above the circus crowd spreading out beneath him, the people slowly getting smaller and more silent as the aviator becomes one with the mists above. Unquestionably he is a very great stylist, but he is so self-absorbed that he seems to actually have a shallow mind and to have been unable to create significant characters with whom we can identify.

I was one of the young editors at Doubleday who wanted to publish *Lolita* in the mid-1950s when it was a banned book—and I still think it is a great novel. Humbert and Lolita's mad scramble across the American wasteland of cheap motels, gas stations, and hamburger stands remains for me one of the most vivid and wonderful descriptions of this country ever written, but it is an outsider's view and a profoundly disdainful one. The only thing that saves it is its lunatic hilarity and headlong push forward, colored by palpable sexuality and the intense preoccupation of smelly desire. Secret, shameful, unacceptable sexuality and the exquisite appreciation of nuance that has become his watermark inform much of Nabokov's work, but no one can now say whether these are enough to earn him a lasting place among the literary classics of the Western world. Nevertheless, he should be read by any student who wants to be familiar with the best stylistic models available.

In this section, then, we have seen four levels of competence in the writing of memoirs—amateur, journalist, professional, and master. Of course infinite gradations of ability and result lie within these limits, but it should be noted that no work less good than that of Mrs. Dana can be expected to find a publisher, and nothing better than that of Nabokov is likely to be written by anybody. Thus this range is the practical limit of what is publishable and of what, in fact, gets published. All of the books made money for their publishers, although *Five Boyhoods* was, I think, a very modest success. Steffens and Nabokov are minor classics, but classics nonetheless. They are representative of the genre as a whole and the student should read them in their entirety as well as reading others like them. Then you should try it for yourself.

BIOGRAPHY

WHEN WE COME TO CONSIDER BIOGRAPHY we reach the dividing line between the amateur writer and the professional, between writing that is done for publication and writing that has been done for other reasons. Biography is written to be published, but it is also true that many writers who do biographies are not professional writers at all, and so some biographies are only marginally professional and their books marginal as publishing projects. Of all the categories of writing it is perhaps biography that is most liable to be not quite up to the standards of other published work. That is why we take it up here as the transition between essentially private writing such as memoir and other fully mature kinds of writing such as history, which has to be professional or it will not see publication.

Why is biography so often marginal? The answer is that some biographers are in a unique position, a position where they have important information that no one else has, and they can use that special placing to do a book that no one else could do. If their writing is not up to regular standards, then the publisher has the choice of taking a book that would not ordinarily be published or else forgoing the publication of information that people may want to have. Basically there are two reasons for people to be in a unique position with respect to a subject; either they knew the subject or they have papers no one else has.

Take, for example, the case of a widow. We have recently seen books by Kenneth Tynan's widow and a book by Dylan Thomas's widow. Tynan, of course, was the brilliant literary and theatrical critic who died young; Thomas was one of the major poets of his age, who managed to drink himself to an early grave. Now it happens that both these widows are very good writers and probably would not have any trouble getting published no matter what their subject was, but it is also true that in each case they have as their subject a famous writer who was very interesting, tormented to a degree, and who died prematurely. Clearly, no one knows either man better than his widow, so they have unique standing. The point to notice is that even if Mrs. Tynan or Mrs. Thomas happened to be a pretty bad writer or not a writer at all, what each knew of her husband's life would be considered worth publishing.

But widows are not the only people in a unique position to write about a subject. Others are in a special position because they have done enough work to become the possessors of a body of knowledge that makes them alone able to produce a biography of a certain subject. In academic circles usually one professor is regarded as the leading scholar on a given subject, so if a publisher wants a book on that subject he usually has to deal with that person. If the subject is obscure, in fact only one person may be able to claim to know all that is available on the subject. A more famous person will command several professors' interest; a great public figure, a whole company's. Since most publishers and most scholars would hardly rush to get a new book on Shakespeare—there being whole libraries of them already—most commonly a person will propose writing a biography about someone whom the writer has special claim to as a subject. The following example may make this clearer:

When I was a much younger editor, I had worked with Harold McCracken on very successful books he had done about Frederic Remington and Charles M. Russell, books that had established him as the leading expert not only on those famous painters but on the art of the American West as a whole. He came to me wanting to do a book on George Catlin, the Indian painter, whose reputation was at the time in eclipse. Catlin's notebooks about his travels among the Indian tribes in the 1830s were easily available in their old published form, his pictures were due for a revival since the Smithsonian Institution was then engaged in cleaning them and planned to display them more, and it seemed right for a new generation to learn about him. I agreed, and we published a very successful book, but it was not because of any felicitousness of McCracken's prose. Here is a sample:

> Although George had no formal training in art, and very meagre funds, he went to Philadelphia in 1823 with the determination to make painting his life's profession. What he lacked in formal training was more than over-balanced by his natural talent and by a magnetic personality which always won him warm friendships among the most intellectual and prominent persons with whom he came in contact. Almost immediately he was admitted to the comradeship of such distinguished Philadelphia artists as Thomas Sully, John Neagle, Charles Wilson and Rembrandt Peale and others. He was not only fortunate in making friendships with the right people, but in keeping them with mutual devotion and respect. Throughout his life, he was counted a most stimulating friend by many of the most notable statesmen and scientists of the period. When he went to Europe he was received into the company of Queen Victoria, King Philippe of France and the King and Queen of Belgium. His normal state of financial insecurity made little difference to his intimates.

Now this is flat, lifeless, and awkward. McCracken was quite aware that he was no stylist, so in the text of the book he used as much as he could of Catlin's own lively journals and letters, but the generally plodding nature of McCracken's prose nonetheless was a drag on what in other hands might have been an exciting book. In this case the other people who were Catlin experts were no better writers than McCracken and had not done the work he had done, had no established name as he had, and in any case were not my authors. Therefore, if I wanted to publish a book on Catlin I had to accept the level of writing that McCracken was able to bring to his subject, or not have a book.

McCracken was a friend and we were very close, and he was, in fairness to him, acutely aware of his own deficiencies. He proposed, in fact, that I rewrite his prose and become co-author with him on this book, but I refused since I didn't have the time and knew that I wouldn't improve the writing enough for it to make all that much difference. Thus in this book, as in not a few other biographies, the level of the prose was not what mattered, and writing that would ordinarily not be deemed publishable was in fact published.

In another case a writer may have access to papers that are not available to others. Sometimes he can acquire that access through sheer hard work, but most often he has gained the confidence of family members who control the papers, or has a special relationship with a library or foundation that owns the papers or holds them in trust. Knowledge, as usual, is power, and access to the papers that provide that knowledge also confers power. That, by the way, is why unauthorized biographies of living people are so often unsatisfactory: without the cooperation of the subject or his family or friends, the writer is so limited in what is available that the result is often weak, shallow, or plain wrong. It is also why the papers of Sigmund Freud, Dr. Martin Luther King, Jr., and other significant figures become virtual battlegrounds among the different people who are trying to gain control over their documents.

It is very important to remember at this point that what we are considering in this book is writing *for publication*— not writing for academic advancement, for kudos from literary critics, or for mere pleasure. This is the question the student wants answered: "Is what I am doing publishable?"

In the case of biography, the rules are different, so the answer to the question depends less than usual on the quality of the prose. Who you are talking about and how you place that person in context are the primary considerations.

Biography thus covers a very wide spectrum of writing ability and intimacy with its subject—one of the widest of any genre. But since it also forms one of the major categories of publishing and serves as one of the principal determinants of how we see our world, we should perhaps look at its history before we even start considering examples.

From the earliest times, the character and actions of a single person were understood to be of the greatest importance, and some classical writings bring to life incidental portraits of people, even though the picture may not be anywhere near complete or what we would now call biography. Plato's depiction of Socrates, for instance, remains vivid today; probably since their composition more people have read Plato's works than those of Aristotle because Plato uses real and understandable people in his dialogues while Aristotle keeps the discussion dry and theoretical.

Plutarch, who wrote in the first century A.D., established individual biography as a major form, although even in his works it remains a mixture of elements. Consider Plutarch's account of the life of Numa Pompilius. Here the Romans, having suddenly lost their king, Romulus, gather to name a successor:

> Consultations being accordingly held, they named Numa Pompilius, of the Sabine race, a person of that high reputation for excellence, that, though he were not actually residing at Rome, yet he was no sooner nominated than accepted by the Sabines, with acclamation almost greater than that of the electors themselves.
>
> The choice being declared and made known to the people, principal men of both parties were appointed to visit and entreat him, that he would accept the administration of the government. Numa resided at a famous city of the Sabines called

Cures, whence the Romans and Sabines gave themselves the joint name of Quirites. Pomponius, an illustrious person, was his father, and he the youngest of his four sons, being (as it had been divinely ordered) born on the twenty-first day of April, the day of the foundation of Rome. He was endued with a soul rarely tempered by nature, and disposed to virtue, which he had yet more subdued by discipline, a severe life, and the study of philosophy; means which had not only succeeded in expelling the baser passions, but also the violent and rapacious temper which barbarians are apt to think highly of; true bravery, in his judgment, was regarded as consisting in the subjugation of our passions by reason.

He banished all luxury and softness from his own home, and, while citizens alike and strangers found in him an incorruptible judge and counsellor, in private he devoted himself not to amusement or lucre, but to the worship of the immortal gods, and the rational contemplation of their divine power and nature. So famous was he, that Tatius, the colleague of Romulus, chose him for his son-in-law, and gave him his only daughter, which, however, did not stimulate his vanity to desire to dwell with his father-in-law at Rome; he rather chose to inhabit with his Sabines, and cherish his own father in his old age; and Tatia, also, preferred the private condition of her husband before the honors and splendor she might have enjoyed with her father. She is said to have died after she had been married thirteen years, and then Numa, leaving the conversation of the town, betook himself to a country life, and in a solitary manner frequented the groves and fields consecrated to the gods, passing his life in desert places. And this in particular gave occasion to the story about the goddess, namely, that Numa did not retire from human society out of any melancholy or disorder of mind, but because he had tasted the joys of more elevated intercourse, and, admitted to celestial wedlock in the love and converse of the goddess Egeria, had attained to blessedness, and to a divine wisdom.

The story evidently resembles those very ancient fables which the Phrygians have received and still account of Attis, the Bithynians of Herodotus, the Arcadians of Endymion, not to mention several others who were thought blessed and beloved of the gods; nor does it seem strange if God, a lover, not of horses or birds, but men, should not disdain to dwell with the virtuous and converse with the wise and temperate soul, though it be altogether hard, indeed, to believe, that any god or daemon is capable of a sensual or bodily love and passion for any human form or beauty. Though, indeed, the wise Egyptians do not unplausibly make the distinction, that it may be possible for a divine spirit so to apply itself to the nature of a woman, as to imbreed in her the first beginnings of generation, while on the other side they conclude it impossible for the male kind to have any intercourse or mixture by the body with any divinity, not considering, however, that what takes place on the one side, must also take place on the other; intermixture, by force of terms, is reciprocal.

It is worth taking the time to consider this extract with some care. It contains what we may suppose is hard fact—who Numa's father was, his having been the youngest of four sons, and when he was born. It includes with equal weight what is acknowledged as hearsay—"She is said to have died." In some respects it is critical and objective in a very modern way, but it also accepts as a given not only the existence of a certain kind of deity but that deity's particular nature—"nor does it seem strange if God, a lover, not of horses or birds, but men." Clearly evident in these ancient fables are the origins of the Christian doctrine of the immaculate conception. At the same time, both Plutarch and the modern reader notice the obvious contradiction in the idea that the gods could mate with a woman but that it was impossible for "the male kind to have any intercourse or mixture by the body with any divinity," Plutarch tersely dismissing the lack of symmetry with "intermixture, by force of terms, is reciprocal."

Thus we have here everything all at once—facts, hearsay, fables, theological debate, explanation, character sketch, moral instruction, and the general course of Roman history. It is in a way completely unmodern, but basic to it is the critical attitude and the distance that the writer feels from his subject that was later to become the first necessity of the modern biographer's position. Since moral instruction was actually Plutarch's basic aim, we may suppose that Numa's exemplary character is to some degree Plutarch's own construct (Numa's selfless devotion to the gods did not in fact prevent him from accepting the throne in Rome, as Plutarch duly tells us); even so, he is generally fair-minded. Nothing like his biographies were to be written again for some fifteen hundred years.

Biography as we understand evolved gradually. Before it took on its modern form, a few autobiographies appeared that were to become milestones of the literature of the Western world. The *Confessions* of St. Augustine, written around A.D. 400, survived and were read throughout the Middle Ages. When the Renaissance dawned, the *Autobiography* of Benvenuto Cellini (1500–1571), which was first printed in 1728, became one of the most important documents from the sixteenth century. Cellini was the consummate Renaissance man, daring, adventurous, breathtakingly skilled at the metalmaker's art, and completely uninhibited and egotistic in his writing, which reads like a picaresque novel.

In the late eighteenth century, two of the great landmarks of Western literature open the modern era: Jean-Jacques Rousseau's *Confessions,* published in 1781 and 1788, were to become one of the most widely read books of our literature, and James Boswell's *Life of Samuel Johnson, LL.D.* was to establish attitudes about biography that have lasted to this day. Each book is well worth reading now, and each one has not only had enormous influence but has also engendered a great mass of recent scholarship. Rousseau evidently considered no emotion or inner feeling too obscure or outrageous to be recorded utterly frankly, and Boswell plainly found nothing Johnson, that "great man," did, said, or thought too inconsequential to escape being carefully recorded. Thus the inner man as well as the outer events and trappings become the subject of the biographer—with nothing left out, nothing escaping notice, and nothing forbidden. The unstated principle of these biographies is that the subject's life should be completely exposed so as to be completely understood. That principle, for better or ill, remains with us today.

Present-day biography, however, cannot be really understood without taking note of two great revolutions in the writing of biography that were brought about first by Lytton Strachey and then by Sigmund Freud. It is worth looking at each in turn.

Biography in the nineteenth century was typically exhaustive, laudatory, and dull. In his preface to *Eminent Victorians,* Strachey criticized such works and explained his own method:

> With us, the most delicate and humane of all the branches of the art of writing has been relegated to the journeymen of letters; we do not reflect that it is perhaps as difficult to write a good life as to live one. Those two fat volumes, with which it is our custom to commemorate the dead—who does not know them, with their ill-digested masses of material, their slipshod style, their tone of tedious panegyric, their lamentable lack of selection, of detachment, of design? They are as familiar as the *cortege* of the undertaker, and wear the same air of slow, funereal barbarism. One is tempted to suppose, of some of them, that they were composed by that functionary, as the final item of his job. The studies in this book are indebted, in more ways than one, to such works—works which certainly deserve the name of Standard Biographies. For they have provided me not only with much indispensable information, but with something even more precious—an example. How many lessons are to be learnt from them! But it is hardly necessary to particularise. To preserve, for instance, a becoming brevity—a brevity which excludes everything that is redundant and nothing that is sig-

nificant—that surely, is the first duty of the biographer. The second, no less surely, is to maintain his own freedom of spirit. It is not his business to be complimentary; it is his business to lay bare the facts of the case, as he understands them.

And Strachey was as good as his promise. Here is how he introduces us to Florence Nightingale:

> Everyone knows the popular conception of Florence Nightingale. The saintly, self-sacrificing woman, the delicate maiden of high degree who threw aside the pleasures of a life of ease to succour the afflicted, the Lady with the Lamp, gliding through the horrors of the hospital at Scutari, and consecrating with the radiance of her goodness the dying soldier's couch—the vision is familiar to all. But the truth was different. The Miss Nightingale of fact was not as facile fancy painted her. She worked in another fashion, and towards another end; she moved under the stress of an impetus which finds no place in the popular imagination. A Demon possessed her. Now demons, whatever else they may be, are full of interest. And so it happens that in the real Miss Nightingale there was more that was interesting than in the legendary one; there was also less that was agreeable.

Today, of course, we have little trouble accepting Strachey's theory that Florence Nightingale suffered all her life from extreme feelings of guilt, and that what drove her to such labor was an attempt at atonement for the depths of her feelings. When this book was published, however, Freud's ideas had not penetrated the popular mind, so Strachey's view of one of the greatest heroines of the Victorian era was taken to be scandalous and defamatory. Here was the biographer as debunker—the cynical and ironical writer puncturing the balloon of the public reputation of famous people. We are now more accustomed to the idea that our heroes may not in fact really be *sans peur et sans reproche,* but then things were different. After Strachey, biographers could no longer merely collect facts and build up admirable pictures. His goal became their own: short, incisive, critical, and well-written works.

The influence of Freud, one supposes, hardly needs much elaboration. As his ideas and his writings became the common stock of educated people, any biographer had to be able to deal with his subject in Freudian terms; in fact, whole biographies were written in no other terms. If Freud's ideas were both revolutionary as well as enlightening, they were also a bit more elusive and more open to interpretation than might appear on the surface. A Freudian may say that Florence Nightingale was guilt driven, and that certainly seems to be the case, but what was the origin of the guilt? Strachey says that by the time she was six, Florence was showing her characteristic symptoms: "Why, as a child in the nursery, when her sister had shown a healthy pleasure in tearing her dolls to pieces, had *she* shown an almost morbid one in sewing them up again?" Well. Do, in fact, most little girls show a healthy pleasure in tearing their dolls to pieces? Would it be more sophisticated to think that there was a good deal of suppressed rage in the Nightingale household and that the two little girls were reacting to the same circumstances but each in her different way? And, having asked *why* Florence sewed up dolls rather than tore them apart, do we get an answer? No. Freud has not yet impressed his ideas on Strachey's mind. But ten or fifteen years later the story would have been different. A biographer would not have been able to ask that question and then leave it there unanswered.

Although the heyday of the Freudian biography has come and (thank goodness) gone, no present-day writer and certainly no contemporary biographer can fail to be aware of the great Freudian revolution in the understanding of human motive and action. People whose biographies are worth writing and publishing are not the usual dull folk that make up the great mass of citizens; they are much more likely to be quirky, driven, and exceptional in both their lives and their true motives. An easy familiarity with such ideas as the unconscious, sublimation, repression, compensation, and symbolic role-playing are now the standard equipment of a biographer, as common and necessary to that occupation as a hammer and nails are to a carpenter. That noted, it should also be said that it is no longer considered necessary to display that knowledge.

Before we consider the full-dress biography, we should take some notice of the shorter form that can be called the sketch or profile—the form that was first perfected by Plutarch, revived by Strachey, and now epitomized by *The New Yorker* "Profile." The brief biography usually makes no claim of completeness, nor does it attempt to place the subject in a larger context, thus avoiding one of the great dilemmas that faces the biographer, and a subject to which we will return. For the moment, we should note that *The New Yorker*'s "Profile" is usually either highly laudatory, as in a sketch such as "The Most Unforgettable Character I Ever Met," or is designed to puncture an inflated reputation. The best of these profiles were all in the nature of a Strachey piece—factually accurate but devastating in their exposure of the reality behind the pretension. The profiles of Henry Luce, Ben Sonnenberg, and Lord Duveen were among the best of their kind, and each was strongly in the debunking tradition, although the means used varied.

The profile of Henry Luce by Wolcott Gibbs, which appeared in the November 28, 1936, issue of *The New Yorker*, was one of the sharpest ever. Using that breathless, efforty, arch reaching for high seriousness that characterized *Time*, which Luce published, to parody that magazine, Gibbs took Luce, who was already rich, pompous, and presumptuous, down a peg. I have heard that Luce never really got over it.

For the profile in the April 8, 1950, *New Yorker* of the outstanding public relations genius Ben Sonnenberg, Geoffrey Hellman, with Sonnenberg's enthusiastic cooperation, decided to do a meticulous inventory of Ben's mansion on Gramercy Park. He merely went through the place and listed the hundreds of monogramed sheets, initialed towels, engraved glasses, embossed place mats, polished matched sets of solid silver tableware, painted boxes, decorated plates, expensive bric-a-brac, lamps, pictures, costly rugs, rare antiques, shelves of leather-bound books, and elaborate window hangings. This gross display of the lavish accumulation of the classic parvenu was enough to put Sonnenberg down as an upstart without taste or standing, a vulgarian exposed. To Sonnenberg it was the classic case of the show-business personality saying to the newspaper critic, "I don't care what you say about me as long as you get my name spelled right." The master publicist knew perfectly well that *The New Yorker* crowd thought they were making fun of him, while he knew that his clientele would double because he had been thought worthy of inclusion in that sophisticated magazine.

Writing the profile of Lord Duveen, which appeared in *The New Yorker* in parts from September 29 to November 3, 1951, presented S. H. Behrman, its author, with a problem. Although Duveen was widely believed to be an amiable crook and flashy con man, his shadier activities were unverified; so in his very long account of how Duveen talked the Robber Barons of the day into buying Europe's most expensive paintings Behrman had to avoid any litigious statements. Later published as a book, Behrman's light-hearted and deftly written profile made Duveen's efforts seem a charming game while it delicately poked fun at American philistinism; as a result, it was at once acceptable to a wide public and proof against libel judgments. Thirty-five years later, proof of Duveen and his art expert Bernard Berenson's dealings came out in other books, but those "revelations" fell a bit flat since any perceptive reader of Behrman's profile had known it all for years.

There is every reason to believe that the profile will continue to be useful and the preferred biographical form among journalists; there will always be inflated egos to prick, and for such jobs a whole book is far too lengthy. It should not, however, be tried by the amateur. Any type of short biography is difficult to get right, but since the under-lying motive of profiles like those in *The New Yorker* is, after all, often malicious, the authors of such sketches are especially vulnerable to attack themselves. This means that the writing must be of a high order, the research completely accurate, and the presentation subtle. Most readers of this book will not be ready to try such a task, but as long as mere presentation of fact in a friendly way is all that is intended, the two- or three-page sketch can be good practice for the longer biography.

Let us now start with an example of what we will label *good*. This is from *Henry Flagler*, by David Leon Chandler.

Thus, when the nineteenth century began, it was known in America, England and France that a substance called petro-leum flowed from springs scattered throughout the Appala-chian forests. Oil had medicinal value, burned freely, gave off a strong but smoky light and was useful as a grease. But, be-cause its odor was so offensive, many doubted it would ever be widely used. This problem was solved in the late 1840s when Samuel Kier, who owned some salt wells in western Pennsyl-vania, discovered that different components of rock oil had dif-ferent boiling points. By controlling the distillation, he could remove much of the odor and smoke problems, and obtain kero-sene, naphtha, lubricating oils and other products. Kier's labo-ratory became the world's first refinery.

Kier had found a use for oil. It would illuminate the world. Compared to lamp oil derived from coal and other sources, petroleum was superior in every way. It was cheaper, it burned clearly and brilliantly, and it would last much longer. It was also the best lubricator for machinery ever known. It didn't congeal in any weather and, unlike other oils, didn't become filthy through use.

The only snag was that the product was in short supply, obtainable only by the various skimming methods.

It was, that is, until August 1859, when the history of the world was changed by a 40-year-old jack-of-all-trades named

Edwin Drake. Drake's accomplishment was to use salt-mining equipment and drill a well beside Oil Creek, 15 miles above its confluence with the Allegheny River. From somewhere below ground, he pumped up oil and as far as anyone knows, it was the first time ever that man had tapped a subterranean supply of petroleum. It was a vast step forward. It meant that oil could be secured in large quantities, and men flocked to the oil fields. Drake's discovery created a storm of excitement and lured a swarm of oilmen, roustabouts, wildcatters and get-rich-quick artists who built a forest of derricks in the desolate region. The boom was on and fortune hunters poured forth in streams.

At the time Drake struck oil, 30-year-old Henry Morrison Flagler was living in central Ohio, about 100 miles west of Oil Creek, two days' travel.

Now, curious as to what it was all about, he stood on a hill gazing down at the creek.

In the spring of 1859, Oil Creek had been bordered by meadows strewn with wildflowers. By winter 1859, when Henry arrived, Oil Creek had turned brown-gray and along a two-mile stretch of it were hundreds of wooden derricks jammed together over oil wells. The spread of wooden derricks and open vats and flimsy shacks almost crowded the farmhouses out of existence. The oil, wasted by primitive drilling methods, had laid vast sheets of shimmering scum over the creeks and lakes.

Henry walked down the hill to talk with the oilmen.

He was a lean, handsome figure. A young captain of cavalry, you might say, trained to ride the field. Excellent head; strange violet-blue eyes; short dark hair parted on the side; straight, classic nose; cleanly shaven face. Picturesque as a stage idol. But a likeable man despite his good looks; a ready and brusque talker who seasoned his ways with philosophy, reflection and a fine sense of humor. A man uncommonly in sympathy with human nature. But there was also a distance.

There was a curious sense of difference rather than mere aloofness. There was no superciliousness, no impatience, no hint of superiority; yet you were subtly made aware that he was alone, by himself.

After becoming acquainted with him, you would find a man who talked freely, yet never freely enough; who answered everything but volunteered nothing. Unlike his friend John D. Rockefeller, Henry Flagler was not a man perennially on his guard. He was calm and kindly; never distant—yet always at a distance.

As he stood on the hill gazing down at Oil Creek that winter day in 1859, Henry Flagler was thinking that business could be done here. His expression was a perfect portrait of confidence.

Now what is to be said about this? In the first place it is a biography of a man who, although he played a large part in both the early American oil business and then in the development of Florida, has largely been forgotten by history. An obscure biography published by The University of Georgia in 1949 never made much of an impression, and so Mr. Chandler had that rare opportunity—to write a biography of an interesting and important figure who has been neglected and to do it with a wealth of material from family sources that makes certain that no other biographer can ever learn more or substantially contradict what he says. This is what every biographer wants. The cooperation of all who have information and most of the family papers easy at hand—in this case in the Flagler Museum—mean that he should be able to produce a book that is both authoritative and full of fresh facts. As a result, *Henry Flagler* must be considered *good* because it is indeed full of information that will be new to the reader and of stories that are in themselves unusual and intriguing—a sort of whole new chunk of American history. One would think that it would be just this sort of book that would sell well, get big first-rate reviews, and please everyone. It didn't. There was something missing.

Thinking about the excerpt we have just read, what do we see? Does the author have a penchant for clichés? It would seem that he does. Drake's innovation was a "vast step forward"; a discovery creates a "storm of excitement"; the oilmen built a "forest of derricks"; "fortune hunters poured forth in streams."

Does he also have a problem with characterization? It would seem that, although he tries very hard, we don't really get a sense of what his man was actually like except that he was handsome but self-contained.

Does the author seem to have a tin ear for words? I think he does. Take what he says about who was lured to the fields: "a swarm of oilmen, roustabouts, wildcatters and get-rich-quick artists." This stopped me because I thought a roustabout was a circus worker who put up and took down the tent, and so I looked it up. The primary meaning of *roustabout* is a deckhand or dockyard worker; its secondary definition is a casual laborer, sometimes in the oil fields; it is less frequently used to mean a circus worker. On the other hand, *roughneck* means, firstly, any tough or coarse person; and secondarily, a worker, specifically on oil rigs. Doesn't Chandler want to convey the idea that a lot of tough guys showed up in the early days of the oil fields? Wouldn't *roughneck* be better than *roustabout?* Readers and even editors seldom stop to analyze word choice, and I do so only to make a point.

Further, doesn't Chandler want to convey that the early oil fields were a lot like gold-rush camps? Why doesn't he say so instead of using clichés? What are get-rich-quick artists? In a gold camp they would be claim-jumpers, gamblers, convicts, and predatory social outcasts, but such undesirables would form only a part of the population. Were they the same in the oil region? We don't get a sense of it.

And then there is the device of placing the hero on a hill gazing down at the creek. Is this convincing? It doesn't sound as if there is a specific source for this scenario, so it has to be symbolic, and "Henry Flagler was thinking that business could be done here" is obviously made up. Should a biographer use this sort of dramatization or should he say simply that as soon as Flagler got to the oil fields he realized that he could make a lot of money there?

The question about putting thoughts into the mind of a biographical subject is an old and unresolved one, but if Flagler is so enigmatic, would Chandler's dramatization be convincing in any case? Tough, private, entrepreneurial types are notoriously hard to understand, so biographers of such people who keep their distance do rather better than Chandler. A recent biographer of J. P. Morgan by Stanley Jackson, for example, makes little attempt to characterize the man, choosing instead to let the events speak for themselves; the result is far more convincing. As an aside, perhaps, but not a trivial aside, it must be remembered that men like Morgan had an enormous *presence:* Morgan's scowl was famous for inspiring terror in those upon whom it was fixed, and his bulk and attitude inspired real awe—all that before he had even said a word. No biographer of Morgan can get to the essence of the man unless he both understands this power and is able to convey something of its force to the reader. But that is art, and that is why writing biography is hard and so often done indifferently. And it is this lack of art that leaves Chandler's biography of Flagler wanting.

The worst thing about a book such as Chandler's is that although it is mediocre it sates the market, preempting even a good study for a long time to come. If a Lytton Strachey were to suddenly appear at the publisher's desk and say that he wanted to do a job on Flagler, the publisher would ask him to wait about fifteen years and to do someone else in the meantime. The biographer must pick someone whose story could either stand retelling because he was so famous or someone whose story is almost unknown—anyone except a figure whose biography, even a second-rate one, has just been published.

So why do I call Chandler's book *good* when I am so severely critical of it? The answer is that as biographies go, it *is* good. What that means, of course, is that it gives us information we want about the person or the era he lived in at a time when a really good biography, which is very hard to do and is thus quite rare, is unavailable. Nonetheless, we can find better efforts, and next we consider one of them.

One of the recurrent problems of the biographer is the Case of the Inarticulate Hero. I vividly remember meeting an undoubted hero of World War II when I was a young editor. He had been a pilot in the Greek air force when the Germans had invaded Greece in 1941. Since his old biplane couldn't even keep up with the motorized columns on the roads below, he was promptly shot down. As he parachuted from his burning plane, his flying suit protected his body from the fire, but his face and hands were horribly burned by the flames of his burning suit as he floated down. The flames only went out when he landed in a river. He was rescued, but he was in such terrible shape that no one wanted to look at him: his hands and face were mostly burned away.

He used his disfigurement to advantage for his government, however. Having no face and no finger pads, he could not be identified, so after he recovered he became a nonperson, able to collect information for the Greek government throughout Europe without being traced. Well educated, he spoke several languages and could pass for almost whomever he chose. His face was so disfigured that people did not want to look at him, so, like a leper in the Middle Ages, he was shunned and allowed to pass unquestioned. For his bravery, the Greek government sent him after the war to America to have his face rebuilt.

When I knew him he had already had sixteen operations and his face, although taut and somewhat masked by large, dark glasses, was more or less presentable. But the question of *who he was* was no nearer an answer than before. He told me that after each operation he would wait until they would let him look in the mirror to find out what he looked like at that point. He said that each time it was all that he could do not to reach up and pull off the face entirely, like some kind of false rubber mask, because the person he saw in the mirror wasn't himself. Of course I wanted him to write a book, but I never got anywhere. He wouldn't repeat to others what he said to friends. He had no interest in going back over all that painful old ground. He couldn't explain his feelings. He could not write his own story and wouldn't dream of letting anyone else do so.

It seems that the kind of person who has a vivid imagination, sensitive feelings, and an acute self-awareness is simply not the sort of person who becomes a hero. A mountain climber, explorer, fighter pilot, or deep-sea diver, for instance, simply would not do those things if he had a mind that dwelt on the horrible possibilities, on all the things that could go wrong, and on the pain involved in making a mistake. So heroes are usually unimaginative and inarticulate, which is why so many of them, if they are to have their stories come out at all, need a writer. Nowadays "heroes" come from the ranks of pop singers, sports stars, actors and actresses, as well as the usual fighters, generals, and politicians. Most often they take on a collaborator who actually writes the "autobiography." These efforts, especially those about sports stars, tend to be pretty flat and shallow as, indeed, are their subjects. Now and again when a really lively and somewhat complex person, such as Lee Iacocca, is the focus, the matter is different. Then the person may be able to explain in some depth what he does and how he feels; the result can be a very interesting book—and one that becomes a best-seller.

Yeager: An Autobiography by General Chuck Yeager and Leo Janos is a *good* recent example. In the following extract, Chuck Yeager relates how, after he escaped from France after having been shot down in World War II, he was eventually taken to a spot near the Spanish border where he hoped to make his escape.

> "You're at the starting point," the guy tells us. "There's a woodsman's shed about a hundred yards directly ahead. You can use that. But no fires and no talking. This place is patrolled.

Start out at first light. Today is March twenty-third. With luck, you can expect to be in Spain by the twenty-seventh or twenty-eighth." He wishes us well and then takes off in the truck.

We spend what's left of the night shivering in the dark hut. By the first light, we set out in the rain, deciding to at least start out together and see how it goes. By noon, two of us have made it to the timberline in gale winds. The other two are lagging far behind, not even in sight. My companion is a lieutenant, a navigator on a B-24 shot down over France. The French provide bread, cheese, and chocolate in our knapsacks. We eat and wait for the others to catch up. We agree that if they can't hack it and reach us in half an hour, we'll go on without them. My fellow-escapee is big and strong; we wait more than forty minutes, then push on together.

The Pyrenees make the hills back home look like straight-aways. We are crossing slightly south of the central ridge that forms the boundary line between occupied France and neutral Spain. The highest peaks are eleven thousand feet, but we figure we won't get higher than six or seven thousand; the trouble is we are up to our knees in wet, heavy snow. We cross ridges so slick with ice that we cross them on the seat of our pants. At first, we rest every hour, then every half-an-hour; but as we climb into the thinning air, we are stopping every ten or fifteen minutes, cold and exhausted. The climb is endless, a bitch of bitches, and I've got to wonder how many of our guys actually make it across these mountains and how many feed the crows that caw overhead.

We sleep and rest when we can, using outcroppings to protect us somewhat from the constant, freezing wind. Our feet are numb, and we both worry about frostbite. The French have given us four pairs of wool socks. We wear two pair at a time, but our boots leak. By the end of the second day, we're not sure how long we've been up here; by the third day, we wonder if we are lost; late into the fourth day, we're almost ready to give up. We should be near the frontier, but low clouds restrict visibility to less than fifty feet. It's four in the afternoon, and we are so

exhausted that we catnap between each step we take, stagger-
ing like two drunks. I'm thinking that this is the kind of situation that produces fatal accidents, when we reach the top of a
ridge and practically bump into a lumberman's cabin. We approach the front door cautiously, my pistol out, but my finger
is so numb that I doubt I could squeeze the trigger. The place
is empty.

I just crumple on the floor. My partner takes off his shoes and
hangs his soaked woolen socks on the branches of a bush. The
two of us sleep side by side on the bare wooden floor. And while
we sleep, a German patrol passes in front of the cabin. They see
the socks hanging on the bush out front. The bastards ask no
questions. They just unsling their rifles and begin firing
through the front door. The first bullets whine above my head
and thud into the wall; I leap through the rear window, my
friend right behind me. I hear him scream, I grab hold of him
and yank him with me as I jump on a snow-covered log slide.
I'm spinning around, ass over teakettle, in a cloud of snow, and
it seems like two miles down to the bottom of that flume. We
splash straight down into a creek.

Fortunately, the water is deep. I surface and so does my
partner. I grab him and paddle across to the other side. Christ,
he's gray. He's been shot in the knee, and he's bleeding to death.
I tear away his pant leg, and I can't believe it. It looks to me
like they hit him with a nine-millimeter soft nose bullet, a
dumdum, because it blew away everything. His lower leg is
attached to his upper leg only by a tendon. Using a penknife,
I cut off that tendon. In my knapsack is a silk shirt that Ga-
briel's wife had made for me out of my parachute, before I left
their farm to join the Maquis. I tear off a piece and tie it tightly
around the stump. Then I take the shirt and wrap it two or
three times around the stump and tie that. He is unconscious,
but still breathing, and we're pretty well hidden from the Germans up above. I decide to wait till dark and then somehow
drag both of us back up that mountain and get us into Spain.

Night falls early in the mountains that time of year, and

thick clouds bury the stars. I can barely see the reflected ice and snow of the steep mountainside. The going is rough and treacherous, dragging both of us up that steep slope. At one point, not even half way up, I lose both my footing and my grip on the collar of my partner's jacket, and we slide backwards more than fifty feet, slamming against a boulder. If the slope had been extreme, that would have been it for both of us, but it was gradual and we weren't sliding fast. It's very cold, but the low cloud deck prevents the temperature from really dropping and glazing the wet snow into a sheet of ice. And at least there is no wind. I stop dozens of times to hear if my friend is still breathing. The truth is, I would be glad to let go of this one-hundred-seventy-pound bundle, but his breathing is regular, although weak. A few times I hear him moan softly.

I think, "He's the lucky one. He's unconscious." Every muscle in my body is hammering at me. I just want to let go of that goddamn bomber guy and drop in my tracks—either to sleep or to die. I don't know why I keep hold of him and struggle to climb. It's the challenge, I guess, and a stubborn pride knowing that most guys would've let go of him before now, and before he stopped breathing. I keep going on anger, cursing the mountain that's trying to break my hump. The mountain isn't exactly trembling, but getting mad at it at least keeps my blood warmer. It's too dark to do anything but inch up, mostly crawling and hauling. I have no idea how far I am from the top, which is just as well. I decide not to stop and rest; I can't trust myself not to fall asleep and let go.

The strange thing is, I think I did go to sleep. One moment it is night, and the next, I panic, thinking I'm bleeding on the snow. But I check again and see that it is the rosy glow of sunrise firing the world. I haven't let go. It happens that fast; dark one minute, light the next. What happened in between, I'll never know, or care. Because we make it to the top. I can let go of him and stand up. We're on top of a glazed snowcap at sunrise.

I walk to the far edge and look down at a long sloping draw.

Off in the distance, through the mist, I see the thin line of a road that must be in Spain. I'm standing near a rocky ledge and a cluster of dwarf pines. I break off a bough, then go back and fetch my partner. I haul him to the edge, check once more to make sure he's still breathing, then shove him over the side and watch him slide down the draw until he's barely a small dot in the snow. Then I hunch down, holding the bough between my bent knees, just as I did when I roller-skated down the steep hill behind my house, using a broomstick as a brake. I'd sit against that stick, and it kept me from breaking my neck. And that's what I do now. I hunch down as low as I can get, put my weight against that bough, and push off down the draw.

When I stop, I'm only about thirty feet from my partner. I crunch through the glazed snowfield, check him out, then give him another shove. He spins down another twenty feet. The draw slopes all the way to the road, so I keep shoving him down until the last fifty yards, when I haul him to the side of the road. By now, he is so gray that I figure he is dead. But there's nothing more that I can do for him. So, I leave him where the first passing motorist would see him. Then I take off, walking south. (I found out later that he was picked up by the Guardia Civil only an hour or so after I left him and was taken to a hospital where they amputated most of the stump. Within six weeks he went home.)

I walk south for another twenty miles until near dusk I reach a small village and turn myself in to the local police. I don't expect a hero's welcome, but I don't expect to be locked into a small, filthy jail cell, either. I want a hot bath, a hot meal, and a warm bed to sleep in for forty-eight hours; and as tired as I am, I'm just not going to spend this night locked in jail. They don't bother to search me, and I'm carrying my survival kit. It contains a small saw for just this kind of situation. The window bars are made of brass, and that good American steel blade zaps through the brass like butter. I find a small pensione a few blocks from the police station. The police know where I am, but ignore me. I eat two portions of steaming chicken and beans, soak for an hour in a hot tub, sleeping with my head propped on the enamel rim. Then I stagger to the bed and dive into it, asleep before I hit the mattress.

I was still sleeping two days later when the American consul knocked on my door. It was early afternoon on March 30, 1944.

Now this is a real hero telling a real story that only makes him seem more of a hero. But note that it is well written, specific, completely convincing, and so compelling that I felt there was no way to use any of this without using it all, even though it makes for a very long example. And look at what it tells us about Yeager himself. Would you, once safe, hack your way out of a jail to get a bath and a bed? Would you have noticed at a time when your enemies are still trying to kill you that a horrible wound was made with a specific kind of bullet? Would you have hauled what you thought was a dying man over the top of the Pyrenees? Would you have known enough to use a pine bough to brake your slide down an icy slope? No. Yeager is exceptional in a way that can only be understood by thinking about a story like this. Mere analysis will not convey what he is like. And then he was willing to talk and was fortunate enough to get a thoroughgoing professional to do the writing. Here, it has all come together, and the result is remarkable and very popular, a great best-seller of the best kind, doubly satisfying because it is so rare.

The reason *Yeager* is *good* is that it is the best of its kind, but there is little that is problematical or subtle or intellectually difficult about Chuck Yeager. You know what kind of man he is. You know what he will do in any given situation. You know where he fits into the history of our times. The challenge lies in bringing to life a subject who is complex and deep and whose influence is immeasurable. Such a one is Thomas Jefferson.

Jefferson, a great leader and ambiguous man, has been a subject of controversy and wonder from his day to ours. What he thought is at least as important as what he did.

And what he thought cannot be understood without a writer having immersed himself in Jefferson's times, read everything Jefferson read, pondered its importance, and then read everything that his contemporaries wrote about him. It is not a task for a journalist, and it tends to be too much for many people of moderate talents, even if they are serious academics. Here we should consider another book I call *good: In Pursuit of Reason, The Life of Thomas Jefferson,* by Noble E. Cunningham, Jr.

The breadth of Jefferson's intellectual world was strikingly displayed during the bicentennial of the American Revolution in 1976 in the exhibition presented by the National Gallery of Art under a banner that read THE EYE OF THOMAS JEF- FERSON. As this extraordinary exhibition showed, public in- terest in Jefferson as a political figure had been joined by an appreciation of his intellectual versatility and accomplish- ments. Behind the new perception of Thomas Jefferson in the second half of the twentieth century lay a renaissance of histor- ical scholarship that brought the launching of the definitive edition of the rich and voluminous collection of Jefferson's pa- pers under the editorship of Julian P. Boyd and the monumen- tal biography of Jefferson by Dumas Malone appearing in six volumes between 1948 and 1981. Simultaneously, a wealth of specialized scholarly studies enriched our understanding of Jefferson and his age. Indeed, the body of scholarly literature relating to Jefferson has become so extensive that few besides specialists in the history of the early nation can attempt to master it.

The present volume is designed to bridge the gap between public interest in Jefferson and the world of scholarship that has widened our knowledge of the man and his times. In offer- ing a one-volume biography that may interest the informed reader, the scholar, and the student alike, I have been fully aware of the difficulties of the task. Recognizing that in any single volume of reasonable length it is impossible to provide a complete account of Jefferson's long life, complex thought, and many interests, I have been selective. But I hope that I have been fair and representative and that a complete portrait of the man emerges. By the subjects that I have chosen to treat in some detail and the words of Jefferson that I have selected to quote, I have imposed an interpretative framework that every historian imposes on the records of the past, but I believe that the material presented and the analysis provided offer an interpretative biographical portrait that the historical record supports.

Because Jefferson achieved his place in history as a public figure, not as a political philosopher, I have incorporated my account of his political thought into the narrative of his public career, rather than separating his philosophy from the context of the times in which he acted. Throughout his adult life, Jefferson saw himself as pursuing reason, and I have allowed him to present his own ideas in his own terms and, as much as possible, in his own words.

This tells us just what we have and what the condition of Jefferson scholarship is in our time. The book itself is a very good example of what might be called competent academic prose—nothing fancy but nothing questionable. It is not for Cunningham to have Jefferson standing on some hill and thinking thoughts. Quite the contrary. We can be sure that if he says that Jefferson was tired or bored or excited or interested, he knows what he is saying because he took it from a letter that Jefferson wrote at the time. During a pause in his public career, when he was fifty and at home farming at Monticello, Jefferson wrote: "Instead of writing 10 or 12 letters a day, which I have been in the habit of doing as a thing of course, I put off answering my letters now, farmer-like, till a rainy day, and then find it sometimes postponed by other necessary occupations."

It was a time when the great men who had made the revolution kept in touch with each other. They were acutely aware of their own importance and of the serious value of their opinions about what they had done. People kept letters, and the Jefferson papers are an enormous trove. The scholar must pick and choose or find himself inundated. In this case what we have is as good a one-volume treatment of Jefferson as we are likely to have in our generation. The book can be given to the college student with confidence that whatever he gets from it will be the truth as we know it. It is not particularly easy reading and presupposes more than casual interest, but it is honest, reliable, complete, and introduces us to Jefferson's own ideas. It is thus an exemplary case of the book of instruction, and the only reason that it is no better than good lies in its severely sober academic style.

We can now consider an example of what I think of as the *best* in biographical writing. Why is it best? Because its subject is a great and an extremely difficult one: the most fascinating, mysterious, controversial, and consequential figure of our recent history—Lyndon Johnson. A biography of a minor figure is doomed to stay minor itself. A biography of a difficult major figure is likely to borrow controversy. A thesis biography designed to prove a specific point of view about a major figure will never satisfy more than a portion of its readers. A fair-minded but unsparing biography is very hard to do, but in the case of *The Path to Power, The Years of Lyndon Johnson,* it seems to me that Robert A. Caro has done it.

What is this book? Merely the first of a projected three-volume examination of the whole life, this volume takes Johnson from his birth in 1908 to the year 1941. This huge 765-page tome, then, covers no more than Johnson's preparation for emergence into national prominence. In fact, the first sixty-five pages, or about forty thousand words (almost half the length of a regular novel), give us nothing but the history of Johnson's family before his birth.

From there on, the examination is minute, the context carefully and fully drawn, and the personalities and characters of those who knew and had dealings with Johnson richly observed and shrewdly laid out. As we read deeper and deeper into this amazing, incredibly complex, and contradictory person's career, little by little we come to see that the many levels of his personality that made him less than predictable prevent anyone—including Johnson himself—from ever understanding the man fully, but the *aura* around him begins to make sense. The kind of world he lived in, his ways of seeing and working, the expectations and ambitions of those around him all begin to emerge by following the story of the deals, elections, alliances, moneygrubbing, and the subtle and shifting politics that were Johnson's daily bread.

Conveying the power of a work such as this with a short quote is difficult because one of its main effects is its cumulative *weight,* but even a short extract shows clearly that Caro is by no means without resources as a writer. The following single page from an early section of the book concerns the loneliness that Lyndon Johnson's mother confronted in her little farmhouse:

> When Rebekah walked out the front door of that little house, there was nothing—a roadrunner streaking behind some rocks with something long and wet dangling from his beak, perhaps, or a rabbit disappearing around a bush so fast that all she really saw was the flash of a white tail—but otherwise nothing. There was no movement except for the ripple of the wind, unless, by happy chance, crows were cawing somewhere nearby. If Rebekah climbed, almost in desperation, the hill in back of the house, what she saw from its crest was more hills, an endless vista of hills, hills on which there was visible not a single house—somewhere up there, of course, was the Benner house, and the Weinheimer house and barn, but they were hidden from her by some rise—hills on which nothing moved, empty hills with, above them, empty sky; a hawk circling silently high overhead was an event. But most of all, there was nothing human, no one to talk to. "If men loved Texas, women, even the Anglo pioneer women, hated it," Fehrenbach has written. ". . . In diaries and letters a thousand separate farm wives left

a record of fear that this country would drive them mad." Not only brutally hard work, but loneliness—what Walter Prescott Webb, who grew up on a farm and could barely restrain his bitterness toward historians who glamorize farm life, calls "nauseating loneliness"—was the lot of a Hill Country farm wife. Loneliness and dread. During the day, there might be a visitor, or at least an occasional passerby on the rutted road. At night, there was no one, no one at all. No matter in what direction Rebekah looked, not a light was visible. The gentle, dreamy, bookish woman would be alone, alone in the dark—sometimes, when clouds covered the moon, in pitch dark—alone in the dark when she went out on the porch to pump water, or out to the barn to feed the horses, alone with the rustling in the trees and the sudden splashes in the river which could be a fish jumping, or a small animal drinking, or someone coming, alone in the storms when the wind howled around the house and tore through its flimsy walls, blowing out the lamps and candles, alone in the night in the horrible nights after a norther, when the freeze came, and ice drove starving rodents from the fields to gnaw at the roofs and walls, and she could hear them chewing there in the dark—alone in bed with no human being to hear you if you should call.

For me, this is one of the few books that makes the Depression understandable. I grew up in the Depression and what I remember was fear—a fear not so much of actual poverty but of the unknown. People didn't understand *why* the Depression had come. They didn't know when it would end or if, indeed, it ever would end. It was as irrational as a great winter storm and as indifferent as the rain. There was no telling how deep the pit was or where the bottom would be found. Caro knows that this fear was the basic common understanding of anyone who grew up then, and that it was in the back of the mind of anyone who grew up then—including Johnson and all the men who would be in Congress by the time he became president. But anyone born after 1940 would never have been through that and would not know the atmosphere in which an earlier generation had been raised.

Here Caro talks about growing up in Johnson City, Texas:

> The picture is shadowed not only by poverty but by fear. Johnson City teenagers understood why they had to work. "Looking back now on those days, it seems as if everyone just about, was worried about meeting the payments of their mortgage," one says. "I know we sure were." Not having a home—being forced to take your possessions and move, to get into your rickety car, and drive off, God knows where, with almost no money in your pocket—that was the abyss. And in 1924 and '25, many Hill Country families were on the very edge of that abyss, and their children knew it. "We had a sense of insecurity." Emmette Redford says. "With very few exceptions—*very* few—a sense of insecurity hung over everyone around there."

It was this deprivation and this fear that would make Johnson cling to the ideals of the New Deal all of his life; they would also make it possible for him to employ the common understanding of his age group to fulfill the dreams that had been born in the worst depths of the Depression. Caro's achievement here and in many other matters is that he is able to convey all this to readers who have mostly known about such things as the Depression from books, if they have known about them at all. This is a major book about a major figure composed with deep knowledge, massive research, and considerable writing strength.

Johnson is such a daunting subject that it is unlikely that another big biography of him will be attempted for at least another generation or so. Then it will probably be peripheral and specialized, for a lot of the people Caro interviewed will have died and no one else will ever be able to claim such wealth of research. This Johnson book will thus stand with Boswell's life of another Johnson as paradigms of the biographical genre.

No recent biography I know of compares to it, except *The Power Broker*, Caro's study of the master builder of New

York City's great road, bridge, and tunnel system, Robert Moses. However, in that book, Caro somehow never really was able to make clear—to me at least—just how Moses accumulated so much power. Moses was more enigmatic than Johnson, so Caro wasn't able to lay him out on the table and dissect him in the way that he later did the former president. But it is a very good book nonetheless, and if not *best,* then close to it.

What then have we learned about biography? Can the writer aspiring to publication learn from what we have seen so far and emulate it? Yes. Clearly, the first requirement for the biographer is to assemble the facts and give them a structure. A life has a natural structure, for each person is born, is brought up in a way that will shape the whole course of his adult life, participates in various activities that form the interesting and significant portion of his life, and, of course, suffers a decline, and dies.

To be taken seriously today, a biographer must also be completely objective. Even Caitlin Thomas, who is only too well aware of her husband's failings and in fact lays them out without pity, cannot possibly be objective enough to qualify her work as true biography; it is simply a memoir. By the same token, campaign biographies are also not true examples of the genre. They are generally sneered at and ephemeral because they are by definition laudatory and uncritical—more hagiography than true biography. My advice is to stay away from them.

Once the biographer has gathered the facts and assumed an objective position, then the work may take any number of courses. For instance, the biography of a hero may consist only of a relation of incidents in his life but the biography of an artist or politician is incomplete without an analysis of his oeuvre or career. In such cases, the biographer's task becomes quite complex. There is first the life, and then there is the meaning of the life. An author's life, for example, may be notable only for its dullness, so what counts is his writings: as a result, the biographer must perforce become a literary critic. Similarly, if he is writing about an artist or sculptor, then he must know enough to be an art critic. For a scientist, a politician, a general, and especially a thinker, the biographer must, again, be well versed in their areas of expertise as well as a storyteller.

I first started to read biographies as a boy about fifty years ago. In fact one of the first books that really got to me was the biography of a horse—*Smoky,* by Will James; after that, I moved on to stories about explorers, naturalists, and adventurers. As I grew older, I realized that a biography generally gave either the story or the meaning of the story, but very rarely both. It has been thus ever since. I don't think I have ever seen a review of a biographical book that does not observe that the author is strong on facts and weak on interpretation, or else good at both interpretation and placing the subject in a historical context but deficient in dealing with the life itself. It is almost as if a single life were a coin: the biographer could either look at the face and describe that or else turn it over and explain the back, but one person was never allowed to do both.

I have always been an admirer of the American sculptor Augustus Saint-Gaudens and felt somehow that I knew him because various members of my family had known him, but for many years there was little or nothing in print about him. Then two books appeared. One was a conventional life, a biography of the man and his career, that, while giving the facts all right gave no sense of the importance and meaning of his work. The author was no art critic and in fact hardly seemed to understand that what his subject was producing was *beautiful.* But that, of course, is the entire meaning of what an artist does all his life, and if the biographer doesn't see the beauty and convey it, then his book is always going to be thin, unsatisfactory, and flat. And so it was with this book.

It was only a year or two later that another book appeared: *The Work of Augustus Saint-Gaudens* by John H. Dryfhout. This was a beautifully printed art catalogue—

scholarly, meticulous, complete, well photographed, and informative. Although it did nothing to place the artist in the context of the larger history of American art and told us little or nothing about what influenced his artistic growth or formed his vision, the book and its pictures did give us the work itself, and we may by looking at it decide for ourselves if we feel its power, thrill at its subtle attractions, and wish we had an example of our own to look at all day, every day.

I feel that way about his *Diana,* his second version of the weathervane atop Stanford White's Madison Square Garden that was installed in 1894. I think she is glorious and nothing would please me more than to look at her every day, and I think that she is probably the most appealing statue that has ever been cast in America—but you would never know from either of these books that Saint-Gaudens ever did anything that had to do with people's emotions. That is always the trouble with a book about an artist. Art is emotional, so if the writer doesn't feel the emotion or convey it, his book will always be wanting.

It is the same with a great politician. Lincoln's saving of the Union was a historical event of the very greatest consequence, but people still tell us almost everything there is to know about Lincoln except that he saved the Union. One only need imagine that the North American landmass was now in the same political condition as Central America, with tiny warring states constantly preoccupied with matters that only serve to keep them in their Balkanized condition, to realize what a disaster it would have been for the Southern states to have succeeded in setting up a separate state. The greatness of America today lies exactly in its being a working Union of enormous size. A European Union to rival that of America is still a generation or so away. If Europe had been unified in 1865, would the great wars of the twentieth century have occurred? Even now, with only the Common Market in place, is a great European war thinkable? It only takes a few questions such as these to see the importance of union. Whether or not a biographer of

Lincoln should explain his historical importance in those terms is not for me to say, but the biographer who ignores such questions will be doomed to writing a second-rate book.

If these thoughts are not enough to sober the writer thinking about attempting a biography, there is another problem that must be solved before starting on any book, one we touched upon lightly in our comparison of Flagler's and Jefferson's stories: "dramatization." A biographer must choose whether or not he is going to place thoughts in his subject's mind, record conversations that *might* have taken place, or stick strictly to the known facts. Facts are dry and hard to make vivid. Thoughts and conversations have appeal, life, liveliness. Which to deal with is always a dilemma, but the writer can avoid neither the choice nor its consequences. All I can say is that if a biography is going to be taken seriously it *must* deal only with verifiable facts; if this costs color and appeal, that is simply too bad. A book can be fiction or nonfiction, but not both. The attempts to "bring history alive" by writing historical novels such as Gore Vidal's *Burr* only debase history for the serious student and leave the person reading them for entertainment unsatisfied. Perhaps that's why historical novels seem to sink out of sight rather quickly while serious biographies, if they are responsible, tend to last. We will discuss fiction later on, but for now I urge the would-be biographer to shun dramatization as he would the harlot on the corner: attractive to be sure, but possibly fatal.

Biography, then, is a very wide genre, perhaps the widest. It can range from a single-page synopsis of the facts of Shakespeare's life all the way to a multivolume compilation of everything that is known about some third-rate writer who shouldn't even be mentioned in the same sentence with the Bard. It can be a flat recital of fact or a deep and subtle examination of intricate and slippery ideas. Its interest depends not so much upon the skill of the writer as upon the importance of the writer's subject, and it thus forms a bridge between the amateur writer and the creator of literature. At its best, biography becomes literature and illuminates the figure as well as the spirit of his age. Even if it does not measure up to the best examples, a biography is worthwhile if it gives pertinent and otherwise unavailable information. The student thinking about publication could well find that writing biography is a path that leads to that goal.

HISTORY

IF IT IS A LONG ROAD from writing a diary to being able to write a biography, then the journey from biography to history is longer yet. It is, in my view, by far the most difficult kind of writing and thus is rarely done well. The ability of historical writers is at least as wide-ranging as that of biographers, but even indifferent history is much harder to write than almost any biography. History is, after all, thousands upon thousands of biographies all rolled together and summarized and synthesized to make a single coherent story. As a result, for practically any subject that the writer may pick, the amount that must be learned before the project can even begin is enormous.

At the very least the historian is expected to "know his subject." Since any subject, whether general or highly specific, will have a huge mass of material available on it, the historian must first find out what is there, choose what is important, relevant, and to be trusted, and then decide on a scheme for handling it all. It is impossible to avoid having some bias, for the mere act of choosing what to take into account will in itself constitute a judgment on the material. Even if the historian considers himself fair-minded and impartial, all his cultural attitudes and expectations will affect his interpretation of the facts, albeit subconsciously, and thus shape his study. Thus all history reflects the culture of the writer, but the history that the writer has read has helped to form that culture. So even though it may seem odd to take up such a difficult genre in this book, history is so important an influence on the worldview of every writer that we must examine the subject even if the reader of this book may be a long way from being ready to attempt it himself.

Every growing child wants to know where we came from, how things got the way they are, and why the world he sees works as it does. The answers to these questions lie in history, and all parents and teachers seem to be aware that what a child learns of history will color his outlook for the rest of his life. The teaching of history is thus immediately political in most cultures, and how it is taught and what is taught are of the greatest interest and concern to the politically active.

When I was young, the Soviet Union's rewriting of Russian history as part of its pervasive attempt at thought control was considered the ultimate proof of Communist evil. The Communists' grotesque manipulation of the facts, their suppression of unpleasant truths, and their fabrication of stories designed to glorify the regime were all offered as examples of everything that is wrong and bad. On May 31, 1988, just as President Reagan was meeting in Moscow with the Soviet leader, Mikhail S. Gorbachev, a story on the front page of the *New York Times* reported that final exams in history in Soviet secondary schools had all been canceled "until textbooks can be brought up to date with the candid approach to history advocated by the Soviet leader." In short, it was time once again to rewrite Soviet history, thus reconfirming that the Soviets know perfectly well that all history writing is political in nature.

If such stories about the Soviets give rise to a certain smug attitude in the American reader, they shouldn't. American history textbooks have been the subject of almost as much political concern as those of the USSR or anywhere else. In America, however, the effect of all the different pressure groups trying to rewrite things to their own satisfaction has not been that American texts have the facts wrong, but that they have become hopelessly bland, sanitized, and prettified.

America Revised, by Frances FitzGerald, was a close look at the deplorable state of the history books that American children were being subjected to. Though her critique was as compelling as what it exposed was ludicrous, one must suspect that little has changed since then.

The sad state of writing in the history textbooks of the present great powers should nonetheless not deter us from trying to trace how history came into being and how it is done properly. To start that, we must begin with the first, and, some think, still the greatest historian—Herodotus (c. 484–c. 425 B.C.). For his nine books on the Persian Wars, each one named for one of the Muses of Greek mythology, which chronicled the great struggle between the Athenians and the Persians that had taken place shortly before he was born, Herodotus relied on oral tradition, the memory of those eyewitnesses who were still alive, and myth, for to the Greeks *myth* was for the most part a form of memory. He related the incidents of the war, but he also included much else, especially descriptions of foreign people and their customs and beliefs. A recent review by Peter Levi, a professor of poetry at the University of Oxford and the author of *A History of Greek Literature,* of David Greene's new translation of Herodotus gives some sense of how this work continues to affect its readers:

> Herodotus wrote in an easy speaking voice, in language that looked loosely organized but was under the control of a great artist. Herodotus examines man and his choices in a historical setting, which amounts practically to a kind of universal history. It is an enterprise of startling boldness; "it is the record of all the logical possibilities, political and human, that coexist in the human world." Herodotus selects his stories with subtle

care, and the moral weight and momentum of his writing are deliberate. The result is "that the History becomes a pattern, itself a kind of myth." Herodotus gives more sheer pleasure than almost any other writer. You laugh aloud reading him. He has more devices and ways of being entertaining than have ever been catalogued. He can be grand, or ominous, or laconic, or casual, or unexpected. He has a fund of stories without parallel, and a sense of construction that is so fresh it almost seems impromptu until you come to analyze it. His prose was perfected in performance before audiences more diverse and more intelligent than we are. He writes history, let alone geography, like a man walking the tightrope, but his climax really is a climax. It is a thrilling victory (*New York Times Book Review*, 28 June 1987).

Probably at least as important as Herodotus is Thucydides (died c. 401 B.C.), whose *Peloponnesian War* stands as the second great early history. As an Athenian general himself and one who was exiled for surrendering his city to the besieging Spartan commander, Thucydides had firsthand knowledge of the events he chronicled, but his accuracy, his studied impartiality, and his refusal to ascribe the course of events to anything but man's general nature give his history a remarkable modernity.

In a review of Donald Kagan's *The Fall of the Athenian Empire* for the May 22, 1988, *New York Times Book Review*, Oswyn Murray—a fellow of Balliol College, Oxford, author of *Early Greece*, and an editor of *The Oxford History of the Classical World*—talks about Thucydides's accomplishments and the failure of nerve that was at the heart of the Athenian decline:

The psychology of this imperial decline was the central theme of Thucydides, the first and perhaps greatest political scientist, who began writing at the start of the war in 431 B.C. Mr. Kagan is a careful and professional historian, but he lacks his tragic vision, his understanding of human psychology and the advantage of being alive at the time of the events he describes. Thucydides devotes a famous section in his book to the pathology of revolution; he analyzes how the discourse of politics breaks down and moderation becomes the only crime.

Thucydides' proud claim that the history of this war shall be "a possession for all time" and that human nature being what it is, we shall always be able to learn lessons from studying these events. When I read Thucydides I know that this is true.

The reason that these two great historians are so important to us today is that they established history as the record of human events that includes human motives and emotions but entirely ignores such things as vague hearsay, ancient myth, and the notions that the wrath of the gods or divine retribution are part of life. The modern idea of history rests upon the notion of the accuracy of factual reporting, the impartiality of the observer, and a certain broadness of mind in the writer.

What comes down to us, and what must concern the present-day writer as well as his publisher, are these questions: Does the writer know his subject? Does he write well and with a deep understanding not only of the subject but of human life?

At this point we can look at a couple of contemporary examples to see what I mean. In American history, the Civil War was perhaps the most important single event, and it is certainly the most written about. Whole libraries are filled with nothing but Civil War books, and studies continue to be written and published. From a publishing point of view, these books illustrate an important and recurring phenomenon: which is that subjects like this run in cycles of popularity and interest. After World War II ended there was, of course, a tremendous outpouring of books about it, and so in the late forties and early fifties a book on the Civil War would have seemed an oddity. In the early fifties, when I was a young editor at Doubleday, we had great trouble trying to interest people in Bruce Catton's first great Civil War book, *Mr. Lincoln's Army.* Perhaps this was because the wheel had not yet turned, but whatever reason it was true that as the fifties wore on World War II books became a surfeit and interested people less and less, and as that happened Bruce Catton's Civil War books came into their own. From that point, interest in the Civil War held steady into the 1960s as its various centennials were observed, and then the subject once again became one about which it appeared that everything had been said that was worth saying. It is very interesting that twenty years after that we once again see new books appearing on the Civil War. It is a good illustration that there are cycles of fashion in writing and publishing and that is true about historical subjects or any other. A scholar may devote a working lifetime to his subject and there will be nonetheless the right time to publish and the wrong time as well. The serious writer should not concern himself with such matters, but the serious editor must.

In any case we are now back in a Civil War book period, and we shall see how two recent books have been received. The first is *Battle Cry of Freedom: The Civil War Era,* by James M. McPherson. In the *New York Times Book Review* for February 14, 1988, Hugh Brogan, himself the author of *The Longman History of The United States,* writes:

> No doubt someone in the Library of Congress knows exactly how many books have been published on the Civil War, but everyone knows, without counting, why a new one is to be greeted somewhat warily. The Civil War is the most worked-over topic in United States history and one of the most written about in the history of the world. It is therefore a particular pleasure to report that "Battle Cry of Freedom" easily overwhelms all such doubts. It is the best one-volume treatment of its subject I have ever come across. It may actually be the best ever published. It is comprehensive yet succinct, scholarly without being pedantic, eloquent but unrhetorical. It is compellingly readable. I was swept away, feeling as if I had never heard the saga before. It is most welcome.

This splendid encomium was matched by half a dozen reviews in other journals; in fact, McPherson's book was praised wherever it was noticed. A best-seller, *Battle Cry of Freedom* is an example of everything that makes it worthwhile to write and publish. It fulfills the publisher's faith in the basic idea that if a book is good enough, it will always make its way, and if a book is very good, well designed and well made, properly promoted and eagerly received, then it can become a huge best-seller.

In unfortunate and embarrassing contrast to all that, we must consider the reception given *The Generals: Ulysses S. Grant and Robert E. Lee,* by Nancy Scott Anderson and Dwight Anderson. Reviewing this book in the *New York Times* on April 3, 1988, about the "two finest generals this country has produced," Stephen W. Sears, himself the author of *Landscape Turned Red: The Battle of Antietam* and a biography of George B. McClellan, had many reservations about it, but his most stinging complaint is about the authors' lack of accuracy. After noting a lengthy series of errors, he continues:

> This may be the most concentrated example of error, but it is by no means the only one. Names are wrong, dates are wrong, chronology is confused, geography is muddled. There are a dozen errors of fact in the section on Lee's Maryland campaign. Grant is promoted to overall command in the western theater six months before the fact. Lee was not stranded north of the Potomac "for weeks" after Gettysburg. The authors quote a letter in which Lee refers to "Mr. F. J. Hooker" and miss the point that this was Lee's sarcastic barb at his latest federal opponent, Joseph (Fighting Joe) Hooker. Students of the war will cock an eyebrow at such statements as "There was Leonidas Polk, the fighting bishop of New Orleans and early adversary of Grant's, who sought peace after being routed by Sherman at Kennesaw Mountain by walking right into Yankee guns." Polk was killed not by walking right into Yankee guns but by an artillery shell while reconnoitering, and it happened

two weeks before Kennesaw Mountain, which rather than being a rout by Sherman was a decided Confederate victory.

From such evidence as this it must be said that the authors are uninformed about Civil War military history, and it shows repeatedly in the chapters they devote to the war. For anyone writing about America's two greatest generals that seems to me to be a crippling failing.

This kind of review kills the sale of a book—as indeed it should—and makes one wonder whether the people involved in preparing it at Alfred A. Knopf care enough about what they are doing. Knopf, now an imprint of Random House, of the top dozen publishing groups, is supposed to carry with it some notion of quality, but if editors and copy editors can let this kind of thing get by them, perhaps management has not been paying enough attention. It is especially curious that such a publishing failure should come from Knopf since that imprint published at about the same time *The Rise and Fall of the Great Powers,* by Paul Kennedy, which, like the McPherson book, was very well written, carefully edited, and handsomely packaged. It was wonderfully reviewed, and also became an important and influential best-seller.

If your instinct is to blame the authors for a deplorable performance, reconsider. All of us think we know about something or other and can be startled when we discover how shallow our understanding really is. No one actually sets out to write a sloppy book, and certainly the Andersons didn't either. They did what they thought was enough, and though it turned out that it wasn't nearly enough, I think the publishing fault lies more with their editors than with them. However, *The Generals* should stand as a warning and a reminder to all writers that, especially with such matters as writing history, someone will always know more than the author about almost any subject, so "know your subject" is no idle precept. It should also serve as a reminder that writers should not operate in isolation: getting opinions on work-in-progress from friends and colleagues is often a good way to avoid obvious difficulties. Perhaps in this case the authors didn't show their book around enough to other historians before shipping it off to their editors at Knopf. In any case, the whole thing is an illustration of just how important it is to get the facts straight, because if readers detect some inaccuracies they will reject the entire book.

We will shortly consider actual examples of history writing, but first we must consider a special pitfall that lies before the historian that does not seem to be such a danger in any other kind of writing. There is no name for it that I know of and I have not even heard it discussed anywhere; but ever since I suffered from its effects as a student, I have felt keenly that historians must be aware of what I call the "assumption of familiarity" syndrome.

The syndrome can best be understood by considering an example. Let us say that in our history textbook we are considering India after the end of World War I, and we read the following: "Westminster became increasingly concerned as Gandhi's novel tactics seemed to actually threaten the foundation of the Raj, for Britain's hegemony over its entire Empire could be at risk if the Nationalist movement could succeed in India." The book goes on to describe The Government of India Act of 1919, which provided that "within each province the functions of government were divided, under a system known as dyarchy, into reserved and transferred subjects." Now this may seem acceptable and commonplace, but as a student, I found it confusing. What is meant by "Westminster"? Who was Gandhi? What were his "novel tactics"? What does "Raj" mean? What is "hegemony" over an empire? What is an empire? What relations did Gandhi have to the Nationalists? What was the "Nationalist movement"? Why would events in India make any difference to other parts of the empire?

Now all these questions might be asked by a student who

was ignorant of India and of the British Empire, which is what most students are when they were presented with this kind of writing, but they are not trivial questions. I still do not really understand how Britain could control India in any real sense. Here were about forty million distant island people who claimed complete control over a highly diverse agglomeration of at least three hundred million people. How was this? How did it work? No one whose work I ever read even thought about these questions, and I didn't really get any sense of what that was all about until I read George Orwell's essay "Shooting an Elephant" many years later. Even now the establishment and maintenance of British control over India astonishes me.

I think a historian writing for American teenagers should be aware of what ideas are likely to seem odd to the average student. That means that, in the above instance, such terms as "Westminster," "the Crown," and "the British Raj" should have been explained before the narrative got too far along. A lot of historical writing actually makes the assumption that the reader knows a lot about the subject beforehand, but one gets the sense that the writer is not aware that he has made this assumption. Military history seems especially prone to this syndrome, and it is all too common in textbooks. But if the would-be historical writer is aware of the danger, he is sure to write better history.

In any case, we are perhaps now ready to start to think about writing history in terms of *good, better,* and *best.* Let us have a look at a couple of examples.

In *Enterprising Elite: The Boston Associates and the World They Made,* Robert F. Dalzell, Jr., examines the actions and motives of that small group of upper-crust Bostonians who established the great millworks of Lowell and Lawrence in the 1820s and 1830s before branching out into insurance, banking, shipping, and various other enterprises as their millworks expanded. Their association was never formalized and operated mostly as a system of interlocking directories based upon the ownership of stock in the various enterprises—but who was invited to acquire stock in each new business as it arose was hardly decided by public offering. To be allowed to buy stock in either a going business or a new one would have been like being asked to join a very exclusive club indeed, for no one whose motives were in any way different from those of the founding partners would have been deemed likely prospects.

The reason the membership in The Boston Associates was so carefully chosen and elevation to that circle so crucial to worldly success was simply that the members did not operate the larger enterprise strictly to make as much money as possible. Their aim was much more complicated. They wanted to maintain over generations their position at the top of society. This meant that the careful selection of competent managers to care for the social health of each succeeding generation was of the utmost importance, and that continuity and longevity were at least as important as profits. Compare this to the outlook and family histories of entrepreneurs and conglomerators of our own time. Where are the progeny and successors of the famous corporate raiders and buccaneers of the second half of the twentieth century? Interestingly, some hundred and fifty years later, many of the descendants of the great Boston families are still well off, their position in society is still secure, and the practice of selecting only the most competent to manage the family fortunes generation by generation still goes on. It is equally interesting to see how little lasting impact some of our most celebrated accumulators of wealth have in fact had. "Shirtsleeves to shirtsleeves in three generations," my father used to say, and plenty of people still conform to this famous American maxim.

It might be noted in passing that even though this is a pretty short book a consideration of The Boston Associates would have been too much to handle in one magazine article. After all, even highly restricted subjects sometimes do require book-length treatments. For example, a cursory examination of the doings of The Boston Associates could have easily missed the whole point: it was only because Dalzell was willing and able to go into hidden motives that his book is so interesting and so suggestive. He does not ask the larger questions, but there is no reason that we cannot. We have been taught in our elementary economics courses that people as economic units always tend to try to maximize their income. In a capitalist society it is expected that there are rational units—individual people—who behave in such a way, and it is upon this assumption that much of economic theory rests. But what if people do not in fact act that way at all? What if people act to maximize their security and their standing in society? What if acquiring money is not at all an end in itself and people only maximize their incomes insofar as that income represents the achievement of other goals—these goals being impossible to quantify, by the way? How can the economist measure the point at which the larger goal has been satisfied and the economic unit no longer has to seek to acquire more income? These are not in fact idle speculations; they are deep hints that there is a good deal more to economic behavior than you will read about in your economics textbooks. They are also illustrations of why reading history is more instructive than the reading of almost any theory.

In any consideration of what might constitute *good* in the writing of history it seems that to make any sense of it all we have to leap from competent small studies to the larger general histories. These are *good* because they give people a large overview of a huge span of time and space, are less likely to be seriously misleading, and provide a sense of the past that can be grasped by a wide readership. For people to understand the context of where and how they live is very important, and so large general histories seem to me equally important. Each period of history itself seems to view its past through a somewhat different lens, and as most of the older general histories are no longer read, we will limit our consideration to books that are roughly of our own time and have been read by people we might know. Books furthermore must to some degree be considered in relation to their impact. A book, however splendid, that has attracted few readers cannot be considered as important as one that has had a great many readers and considerable influence. Three famous books have had, for example, great impact on the thinking of generations of students, and colored their whole attitude toward historical events. They are: *On War,* by Karl Von Clausewitz, *The Influence of Sea Power upon History,* by Alfred T. Mahan, and *The Significance of the Frontier in American History,* by Frederick Jackson Turner, and their influence is great regardless of whether they are well written or what they say is truly convincing today. Remember that we are considering from the point of view of the publisher, so that famous and influential books must be considered important no matter how they are written.

In the last fifty years or so, then, there have been a number of big general histories that qualify for what we think of as *good.* Perhaps the most notable of these was Arnold J. Toynbee's *A Study of History*, a ten-volume attempt to write the whole history of mankind, which appeared from 1935 to 1954. It was the last great try for a compilation of *everything* and a cause of much astonishment for trying to be just that. First started in 1947 and then completed in 1957, an abridgement in two volumes was published, also in 1957, and this caused something of a sensation in historical circles. The reason was that Toynbee was not only the last historian to try to write all history—he also tried to give it sensible shape by supplying a structural theory to explain it all. This was, to oversimplify, roughly a pattern of challenge and response—or failure to respond. He saw the rise of civilization as a series of patterns of growth and accumulation of power and culture and then of challenges either met or not met followed by disintegration and decline. In short, he thought he could see a pattern in the whole thing that gave the whole some coherence and thus made all of history one great connected story. It should go without saying that this notion was vigorously challenged for other historians were quick to note that it seemed to them that Toynbee wished to put all of history in a sort of straight-jacket, and one that didn't fit. Plenty of historians could discern no pattern in history, and nothing as orderly and neat as he suggested in any case. The merit of those arguments need not concern us here, but it is nonetheless true that since Toynbee no other historian has tried either to write a complete history of the world or to give it a regular and understandable pattern. His work is not much read anymore, but those students who wish to get a sense of what it is all about should get a copy of *Mankind and Mother Earth: A Narrative History of the World,* by Arnold J. Toynbee, which, at only 688 pages long is a manageable introduction to his ideas and his methods.

In our time the only other notable writer who tried to write a whole history of mankind was Will Durant. His *Story of Civilization* was started with *Our Oriental Heritage* and published in 1935 by Simon & Schuster, then a brash new publisher just ten years old and struggling through the worst years of the Depression. It was pop history and never made much effort to present itself as anything else. It was, however, taken up by the Book-of-the-Month Club, which stayed with the series for many years and thus brought the books to a very wide audience. After getting as far as Volume 6, *The Reformation,* by himself, Will was joined by his wife Ariel, and together they produced volumes 7 through 10, which was *Rousseau and Revolution* published in 1967. All these books seem to be good-hearted and inoffensive, and thanks to their wide circulation and the middlebrow nature of the readers to be expected from the club they became sort of the delight of the autodidact. One would have to suspect that they constituted furniture in the shelves of many suburban split-levels, but still I would feel entirely safe in handing one of them to a curious fifteen-year-old.

A distinct cut above the work of the Durants is that of Page Smith, who is not only a professional historian but also confines himself to American history. Years ago, when I was immobilized for some weeks by an operation on my knee, I read the whole of Smith's two-volume biography of John Adams, a work in which he lets Adams and his wife, Abigail, speak for themselves much of the time. They were constant and wonderful letter writers—in fact, both of them wrote better than Smith—so he is correct to give us their own words directly. He is also fair and thorough in giving the context and import of what they say. Nevertheless, it is necessary to care a good deal about John Adams to get through the whole of the two volumes since Smith, although honest and reliable, is no stylist.

The virtues of thoroughness and fair-mindedness are not to be cut-priced, however, for they are what makes Smith's People's History series the solid piece of work it is. Starting with *A New Age Now Begins: A People's History of the American Revolution,* printed in two volumes (2,000 pages even!), and ending with volume six, *The Rise of Industrial America: A People's History of the Post-Reconstruction Era,* Smith leads us with sober authority and adequate disengagement through a wide variety of topics important in the study of American history: politics, religion, education, the blacks, women, the literary scene, the arts, the opening of the west, sports, business, journalism, the classes, and immigration, among others. The treatment of its subjects is not deep and the writing is not notable, but the series does give a lot of interesting, useful information and a sense of what the American past was really like. This is a decent accomplishment and much more than many books can offer, so we should have no hesitation in learning our American history from Smith.

Turning from the merely *good* to think about what might constitute *better,* we come to the point of considering history as literature. The historians who can safely be called *better* will be as well grounded in the basic facts as, say, Page Smith but they will write better, be better able to bring a story alive, and have a deeper insight into human character.

In *History as Literature,* Orville Prescott gives brief samples of forty-nine authors from Herodotus to Bruce Catton selected for "literary distinction and dramatic interest," and they are well worth reading indeed. This anthology is a reliable guide through the vast field of historical writing, which seemingly has few standards. Perhaps the Napoleonic Wars hold less fascination for us today than they did for others fifty or a hundred years ago, so we decide to skip reading G. M. Trevelyan's views on it, but it is good to know that the best historian of the period is there to be read if we wish. In American history such great writers as Bernal Diaz Del Castillo, William H. Prescott, and Francis Parkman are also represented. Some less well established historians are there, too, but only those in the front rank of their profession are included. It is this level of historiography that I would urge the student to read as widely as possible, for although attaining this quality of expression is both rare and difficult, a firm knowledge of the best models is the first step toward such high achievement.

In the 1950s Doubleday published the Mainstream of America series, edited by Lewis Gannett. A notable effort and worth looking into even now, the series rested on the premise that very good established writers, whether their reputations had been made in history writing or something else, and many of them were indeed based on "something else," could if asked write better history than most professional historians. The editors wanted people who were writers first and historians second. The resulting series of titles, which are listed below, were very readable, and the history was no less reliable for that:

The Age of Fighting Sail, by C. S. Forester
The Age of the Moguls, by Stewart H. Holbrook
From Lexington to Liberty, by Bruce Lancaster

Glory, God, and Gold, by Paul I. Wellman

The Land They Fought For, by Clifford Dowdey

New Found World, by Harold Lamb

Men to Match My Mountains, by Irving Stone

The Men Who Made the Nation, by John Dos Passos

This Hallowed Ground, by Bruce Catton

Dreamers of the American Dream, by Stewart H. Holbrook

All these authors were, to say the least, well known and highly regarded writers before they undertook their history volume, but perhaps Bruce Catton was the most celebrated as both a historian and writer. Since we have not used many examples in this section, I include here one from the end of Catton's *This Hallowed Ground:*

> In Washington the great reviews were held as scheduled, toward the end of May. Thousands of men tramped down Pennsylvania Avenue, battle flags fluttering in the spring wind for the last time, field artillery trundling heavily along with unshotted guns, and great multitudes lined the streets and cheered until they could cheer no more as the banners went by inscribed with the terrible names—Bull Run, Antietam, Vicksburg, Atlanta—and President Johnson took the salute in his box by the White House. It was noticed that Sherman's army unaccountably managed to spruce up and march as if parade-ground maneuvers were its favorite diversion. Sherman had apologized to Meade in advance for the poor showing he expected his boys to make; when he looked back, leading the parade, and saw his regiments faultlessly aligned, keeping step and going along like so many Grenadier Guards, he confessed that he knew the happiest moment of his life.
>
> And finally the parades were over and the men waited in their camps for the papers that would send them home and transform them into civilians again.
>
> ... There was a quiet, cloudless May evening in Washington,

with no touch of breeze stirring. In the camp of the V Corps of the Army of the Potomac men lounged in front of their tents, feeling the familiar monotony of camp life for the last time. Here and there impromptu male quartets were singing. On some impulse a few soldiers got out candles, stuck them in the muzzles of their muskets, lighted them, and began to march down a company street; in the windless twilight the moving flames hardly so much as flickered.

Other soldiers saw, liked the looks of it, got out their own candles, and joined in the parade, until presently the whole camp was astir. Privates were appointed temporary lieutenants, captains, and colonels, whole regiments began to form, spur-of-the-moment brigadiers were commissioned, bands turned out to make music—and by the time full darkness had come the whole army corps was on the parade ground, swinging in and out, nothing visible but thousands upon thousands of candle flames.

Watching from a distance, a reporter for the New York *Herald* thought the sight beautiful beyond description. No torchlight procession Broadway ever saw, he said, could compare with it. Here there seemed to be infinite room; this army corps had the night itself for its drill field, and as the little lights moved in and out it was "as though the gaslights of a great city had suddenly become animated and had taken to dancing." The parade went on and on; the dancing flames narrowed into endless moving columns, broke out into broad wheeling lines, swung back into columns again, fanned out across the darkness with music floating down the still air.

As they paraded the men began to cheer. They had marched many weary miles in the last four years, into battle and out of battle, through forests and across rivers, uphill and downhill and over the fields, moving always because they had to go where they were told to go. Now they were marching just for the fun of it. It was the last march of all and, when the candles burned out, the night would swallow soldiers and music and the great army itself; but while the candles still burned, the men cheered.

The night would swallow everything—the war and its

echoes, the graves that had been dug and the tears that had been shed because of them, the hatreds that had been raised, the wrongs that had been endured and the inexpressible hopes that had been kindled—and in the end the last little flame would flicker out, leaving no more than a wisp of gray smoke to curl away unseen. The night would take all of this, as it had already taken so many men and so many ideals—Lincoln and McPherson, old Stonewall and Pat Cleburne, the chance for a peace made in friendship and understanding, the hour of vision that saw fair dealing for men just released from bondage. But for the moment the lights still twinkled, infinitely fragile, flames that bent to the weight of their own advance, as insubstantial as the dream of a better world in the hearts of men; and they moved to the far-off sound of music and laughter. The final end would not be darkness. Somewhere, far beyond the night, there would be a brighter and a stronger light.

Now, what are we to make of this? Does it bring a catch to your throat and the sting of a tear to the corner of your eye? Does it seem to be shameless pandering to the most hackneyed and mawkish of sentiment, an empty promise of a vague hope as childish as it is unrealistic? Is this a sad and noble way to end a book on America's greatest war or is it an overwritten example of "fine writing" that seeks to enlist our emotions where they are neither needed nor appropriate? Well, the trouble is that I think it is all those things, and that is why Catton is so popular with readers and so suspect as a historian, although I think he is, in fact, a scrupulously careful and completely reliable historian. Note that his account of the parade comes straight from that of a contemporary newspaperman and that he even takes care to tell us this. But your average historian can't write like this, and most of them wouldn't dare if they could. The suspicion of Catton's historiography is an example of the tension between the academic world and the world of popular publishing. I think that if our children would rather read Catton, by all means let them. Meanwhile, the professors will hand them the same dull textbooks they always have and continue to wonder why they don't find history exciting.

As each generation must rewrite history through its own particular lens, it is interesting to see that a new history series has now been undertaken by The Oxford University Press under the general editorship of C. Vann Woodward to be called the Oxford History of the United States. *Battle Cry of Freedom,* which we have already noticed, is a volume in this series, and it seems clear that McPherson will do for our present generation what Catton did for his. This is all to the good: a serious student should be able to learn a lot by reading and comparing both writers.

Before leaving a discussion of *better* books, it is perhaps appropriate to notice two big books that have been widely read and influential. The first is *The Rise of the West: A History of the Human Community,* by William H. McNeill. The outline of history McNeill presents did not raise the protest that Toynbee's had because it seemed entirely neutral and open-minded and did not try to impose order where there was none. Here is his introduction to the modern period:

> The key to world history from 1500 is the growing political dominance first of western Europe, then of an enlarged European-type society planted astride the north Atlantic and extending eastward into Siberia. Yet until about 1700, the ancient landward frontiers of the Asian civilizations retained much of their old significance. Both India (from 1526) and China (by 1644) suffered yet another conquest from across these frontiers; and the Ottoman empire did not exhaust its expansive power until near the close of the seventeenth century. Only in Central America and western South America did Europeans succeed in establishing extensive land empires overseas during this period. Hence the years 1500–1700 may be regarded as transitional between the old land-centered and the new ocean-centered pattern of ecumenical relationships—a time when

European enterprise had modified, but not yet upset the four-fold balance of the Old World.

The next major period, 1700–1850, saw a decisive alteration of the balance in favor of Europe, except in the Far East. Two great outliers were added to the Western world by the Petrine conversion of Russia and by the colonization of North America. Less massive offshoots of European society were simultaneously established in southernmost Africa, in the South American pampas, and in Australia. India was subjected to European rule; the Moslem Middle East escaped a similar fate only because of intra-European rivalries; and the barbarian reservoir of the Eurasian steppes lost its last shreds of military and cultural significance with the progress of Russian and Chinese conquest and colonization.

After 1850, the rapid development of mechanically powered industry enormously enhanced the political and cultural primacy of the West. At the beginning of this period, the Far Eastern citadel fell before Western gunboats; and a few of the European nations extended and consolidated colonial empires in Asia and Africa. Although European empires have decayed since 1945, and the separate nation-states of Europe have been eclipsed as centers of political power by the melding of peoples and nations occurring under the aegis of both the American and Russian governments, it remains true that, since the end of World War II, the scramble to imitate and appropriate science, technology, and other aspects of Western culture has accelerated enormously all round the world. Thus the dethronement of Western Europe from its brief mastery of the globe coincided with (and was caused by) an unprecedented, rapid Westernization of all the peoples of the earth. The rise of the West seems today still far from its apogee; nor is it obvious, even in the narrower political sense, that the era of Western dominance is past. The American and Russian outliers of European civilization remain militarily far stronger than the other states of the world, while the power of a federally reorganized western Europe is potentially superior to both and remains inferior only because of difficulties in articulating common policies among nations still clinging to the trappings of their decaying sovereignties.

It is extremely interesting to note that this was written just twenty-five years ago, and although most western European nations are indeed "still clinging to the trappings of their decaying sovereignties," the political unification of Europe is now proceeding apace. The Common Market exists as does a nascent European Parliament and all customs and financial barriers are due to come down in 1992. The beginnings of a common currency are in place, and there is already talk about establishing a Central Bank. So we can see with these small technical steps, which will eventually have to be ratified and followed by formal political arrangements, the United States of Europe is already well in view.

What McNeill's book did in 1963 was to remind its readers, at the time barely recovering from the trauma of the Cuban missile crisis, that in the context of history such occurrences were much less important than they seemed at the time. The Cold War seemed to frame every discussion until one thought about the larger world, the longer time, the underlying strengths of nations and peoples. McNeill opened the politicians' eyes to a broader view than they were accustomed to and thus had, in my view, a significant calming influence in a very tense time.

In our time another book has come along that has already commanded wide interest and some real thought: Paul Kennedy's *The Rise and Fall of the Great Powers: Economic Change and Military Conflict from 1500 to 2000*. The notion that great powers engender their own decline by being over-extended has been with us at least since Gibbon and probably since Herodotus but to have the thesis put into modern terms and with careful scholarship made the message palatable and pertinent to the readers of 1988. Here is how Kennedy describes his book:

The story of "the rise and fall of the Great Powers" which is presented in these chapters may be briefly summarized here. The first chapter sets the scene for all that follows by examining the world around 1500 and by analyzing the strengths and weaknesses of each of the "power centers" of that time—Ming China; the Ottoman Empire and its Muslim offshoot in India, the Mogul Empire; Muscovy; Tokugawa Japan; and the cluster of states in west-central Europe. At the beginning of the sixteenth century it was by no means apparent that the last-named region was destined to rise above all the rest. But however imposing and organized some of those oriental empires appeared by comparison with Europe, they all suffered from the consequences of having a centralized authority which insisted upon a uniformity of belief and practice, not only in official state religion but also in such areas as commercial activities and weapons development. The lack of any such supreme authority in Europe and the warlike rivalries among its various kingdoms and city-states stimulated a constant search for military improvements, which interacted fruitfully with the newer technological and commercial advances that were also being thrown up in this competitive, entrepreneurial environment. Possessing fewer obstacles to change, European societies entered into a constantly upward spiral of economic growth and enhanced military effectiveness which, over time, was to carry them ahead of all other regions of the globe.

While this dynamic of technological change and military competitiveness drove Europe forward in its usual jostling, pluralistic way, there still remained the possibility that one of the contending states might acquire sufficient resources to surpass the others, and then to dominate the continent. For about 150 years after 1500, a dynastic-religious bloc under the Spanish and Austrian Habsburgs seemed to threaten to do just that, and the efforts of the other major European states to check this "Habsburg bid for mastery" occupy the whole of Chapter 2. As is done throughout this book, the strengths and weaknesses of each of the leading Powers are analyzed *relatively,* and in the light of the broader economic and technological changes affecting western society as a whole, in order that the reader can understand better the outcome of the many wars of this period.

This book bids fair to do for the present moment what McNeill did for his generation, which is to open up the eyes of people in politics and policy to a larger perspective and a longer time span. This can only be applauded, and the authors thanked for the depth of their knowledge, the serviceability of their prose, and the breadth of their vision. The student of writing should note that what these men have to offer is the result of vast learning and not facility of expression, but that the expression is adequate for their purpose, and that purpose is of a high order.

If all these books merely constitute *better,* however, what can we think of as being *best?* Here the field of contenders is severely limited, for *best* demands complete mastery of the subject and unsurpassed powers of expression. I can think of only two writers who would without argument fill the bill. In our time there is the medieval historian George Duby, who is represented with a small gem, *William Marshal: The Flower of Chivalry,* and for all time there is Edward Gibbon, whose *The Decline and Fall of the Roman Empire* is generally recognized as one of the greatest books ever written. Let us have a look at each one.

Duby's study reconstructs of the life of William Marshal (1145–1219), the fourth son of a minor knight who rose to become an earl and the regent of Henry, the future king of England. Its picture of Marshal's life and his time seems to us as fanciful as any society in a science fiction novel—a strange, harsh, warlike time when the rigidities of knightly life governed all conduct. Based upon one of the first monuments of French literature, a *chanson de geste* of 19,914 verses recounting the life of William, Duby's tracing of Marshal's rise to power through feats of arms and bravery brings this oddly constrained but violent era to understandable and vivid life. The knight's code depended first upon loyalty—to keep one's word and not to betray one's sworn faith; second, on feats of valor—to do battle and to triumph, conforming to strict laws; and, finally, on *largesse,* or generosity—to keep nothing and to give away all that comes to him. These precepts, and the wish to win the love of women—ladies, that is, or highborn women—are the formula for winning social distinction, and William won more than anyone in his time. Duby's re-creation of the time is based upon a deep, lifelong study of the period and his easy familiarity with its conventions and modes of thought. He slips us into twelfth-century England as easily as if we were reading about yesterday, but real as it was, it is a time so long gone that it seems legendary. Here is our last glance at Marshal:

> Out of the depths of his memory there rose an image from early childhood, from the time when he used to play—even younger than this little Henry—in the arms of the then king of England. Now he was holding today's king in his arms, earthly power at the highest level it could achieve in this world. Apotheosis. For two years he could do what he would. But acting as he had never ceased to act, according to the rules of knightly honor. As a simple knight.
>
> He had never been anything else. A younger son without possessions. Now rich and a baron, but as the guardian of his wife and of her sons. Invested with royal power, but as regent of the under-age king. Without having imagined he would accede to this degree of power. Without being trained to wield it, and without the title to do so which might come to him by blood or by the priestly liturgy. With no other virtue—and those who celebrated his virtues, speaking for him, repeating his own words, expressing what he himself believed, never sought to say anything different—than to be considered the flower of chivalry. It was to this excellence, and to this alone, that he owed his extraordinary elevation. Thanks to that great indefatigable body of his, powerful and skilled in knightly exercises; thanks to that brain apparently too small to hamper the natural bloom of his physical vigor by superfluous reasoning: few thoughts and

brief, a stubborn attachment to the rough-hewn ethic of men of war whose values abide in three words: prowess, generosity, loyalty. And thanks to his longevity above all, a miracle. Have we not touched here on what is essential? In the person of William Marshal, in that indestructible frame, survived the twelfth century of all his early exploits, that century of tumultuous exuberance, of Lancelot, of Gawain, of the Knights of the Round Table . . . The good old days, the days gone by. He could advance calmly toward death, proud of having been the instrument of the final, the fugitive, the anachronistic triumph of honor against money, of loyalty against the state—of having borne chivalry to its fulfillment.

Small and gemlike, Duby's book is *best* because it is unlikely that anyone else will ever make us understand the middle ages as he does.

Gibbon's work is also *best,* but at the other end of the scale, for it is large and magnificent and all-encompassing and unique. First published in six volumes from 1776 to 1788, *The History of the Decline and Fall of the Roman Empire* was at once recognized as a great masterwork and has been on everyone's short list of essential books ever since. Gibbon's disdain for the Christian church and the essential irony of his outlook have made him the special target of clerical hostility ever since—so much so that books are even now appearing on the subject. *The Excellent Empire: The Fall of Rome and the Triumph of the Church* by Jaroslav Pelikan is a modern examination of Gibbon's thoughts compared to the Church Fathers' reactions to the same history—Gibbon seeing in historical events "the triumph of barbarism and religion"; and the clergy, of course, the "rise and triumph" of the Church. It is interesting that John Gross, reviewing the book in the *Times* (February 1, 1988) says of Pelikan that "most of all in his quotations, he makes us freshly aware of the unsurpassed power of Gibbon's historical vision, and the magnificence of his style."

Students of writing and readers of this book should with-

out doubt read Gibbon for inspiration but should also remember that his style is so overpowering that it would be
a great mistake to write as he does. Gibbon can say "as long
as mankind shall continue to bestow more liberal applause
on their destroyers than on their benefactors, the thirst of
military glory will ever be the vice of the most exalted
characters"; or "The various modes of worship, which prevailed in the Roman world, were all considered by the people, as equally true; by the philosopher, as equally false; and
by the magistrate, as equally useful. And thus toleration
produced not only mutual indulgence, but even religious
concord." It is only a completely secure and unself-conscious
mind that can produce this kind of prose; anyone who tries
it now will produce parody, and a peculiarly embarrassing
kind of parody at that. Nonetheless, like the King James
version of the Bible, Gibbon should be read for a sober exal-
tation of the mind and a reminder of the austere grandeur
that can be built upon a record of folly and ruin.

Before we leave our consideration of the writing of history,
we must note that in the past generation or so the field has
been torn between traditionalists and revisionists. The old
mode of historiography, a narrative of the doings of politicians and warriors and of plagues, invasions, and upheav-
als, that had prevailed since Herodotus has been brought
into question. The new historiography insists upon a new
focus, but the revisionists disagree among themselves just
what that focus should be. Since I have no standing in the
field, let me convey this turmoil through the comments of
some people who are more directly involved in the controversy:

To begin with, three kinds of "new" history have
emerged: political, sociological, and psychoanalytic. In addition, the expected point of view has shifted, so that, for
example, the Battle of the Little Big Horn is written from
Crazy Horse's point of view instead of Custer's. Each of

these trends has been explained to some degree in recent reviews.

In his discussion of E. J. Hobsbawn's *The Age of Empire, 1875–1914* in the *New York Times Book Review* in early 1988, David M. Kennedy, the William Robertson Coe Professor of History at Stanford University, briefly traced the emergence of the new history:

> In 1952, E.J. Hobsbawn helped to found a learned journal, Past and Present, whose first issue vigorously rejected "the view . . . that history is merely one damned thing after another." Sharply to the contrary, the editors committed themselves to a "rational and scientific approach to history," one that would analyze the patterns and dynamics of the past, refuse to "separate the study of the past from the present and future" and would employ instead the "historical discipline as an instrument enabling us 'to face coming events with confidence.' "
>
> That scholarly manifesto, with its unmistakably Marxist overtones, energized a remarkable group of British historians, of whom Mr. Hobsbawn, emeritus professor of economics and social history at the University of London, has proved to be one of the most creative and prolific. His works on southern Italian bandits and rural English rebels inventively identified the inchoate antecedents of modern socialist and labor organizations. They were also pioneering studies in the field of social history—the study of ordinary people, the inarticulate masses who were done to, rather than the record-leaving doers who shook states and moved armies—that has so transformed the character of historical scholarship in the last three decades.

In the *New York Review of Books* (May 12, 1988), Michael Kazin reflected on the influence of Herbert G. Gutman, author of *Power and Culture: Essays on the American Working Class,* on the revisionists:

> Herbert Gutman, who died in 1985 at the age of fifty-seven, was one of a small group of older American historians who made the experience of workers, women, and racial minorities central to

the study of American history. In so doing he became a guiding influence for many of the hundreds of younger scholars of the late 1960s and 1970s who were exploring such subjects as slave religion, immigrant family life, and the ideology of artisans. Gutman's own writings concentrated on the blacks and European immigrants who did most of the labor on plantations and in factory towns and cities during the nineteenth century. Drawing on statistics, stories, poems, and his own provocative interpretations of historical events, he gave a version of slavery and industrialization quite different from the rather grim and dry portraits that are still to be found in textbooks.

Gutman was not an academic specialist constantly refining one small segment of the past. He passionately supported writers, inside or outside the universities, who tried to understand people who were once called "the inarticulate" by reconstructing their rich and diverse cultures.

The thrust of the work of these two historians and their followers and students seems straightforward enough on first glance, but following them down the path that they have pointed out, one is likely to find that the idea of impartiality has been left behind. This is frankly history as argument, and, without making any kind of determination of the merits of the argument itself, the reader will perhaps begin to feel that he is reading polemics rather than history as we used to understand it. If you take that to be merely reading history to find the hidden meaning in it, you will likely agree with the authors' underlying argument, but if you think that our common understanding of what history is stands at risk from such readings of it, then you may well be wary. I am. Their "rational and scientific approach to history" carries with it an unspoken and purposeful agenda whether or not the authors admit it; in reading such works it is well to be as careful as possible.

Both the pervasiveness and the subtlety of the problem

were well illustrated by Linda Colley in her critique for the *London Review of Books* (March 17, 1988) of several new books on Victorian England:

> More than fifty years have elapsed since G. M. Young published his splendidly suggestive survey of Victorian England, *Portrait of an Age,* and the confidence and command which enabled that book to be written seem to become ever more elusive. The exponential growth of the academic profession, and the sheer volume of relevant material and accumulated images, have ensured that our detailed knowledge about this period has advanced enormously since Young's day. But knowledge does not always bring understanding. At present, some three hundred and fifty books and articles on 19th-century Britain appear every year. Most of them concentrate on only a limited portion of the period, and on only a particular locality or class or occupation or gender or individual within it. Like Humpty Dumpty, Victorian England seems at times to be in too many pieces ever to be put together again.
>
> Yet there are signs that micro-history is losing some of its appeal. Political history, so long overshadowed by social history, is markedly resurgent. As a result, more attention is now being given to the state and to the nation as valuable units of study. At the same time, scholars are becoming more willing to tackle the long chronological sweep. Insofar as these developments enhance our appreciation of the broader processes of the past, they are much to be welcomed. But they also need to be watched. For there is little doubt that behind some of this revived enthusiasm for collective, national and impressionistic history there is a political rather than a scholarly imperative.

But that is not all that the revisionists have introduced to the writing of history. There are other new perspectives, as Norman Hampson pointed out in the *New York Review of Books* (June 2, 1988) in his piece on four recent monographs on the French Revolution:

In the history of the Revolution an increasingly sterile controversy between rigorous economic determinists and their opponents has given way to a general recognition that class conflict and class incomprehension were one element within a much more complex confrontation of interest and principles. This makes, if not for consensus, at least for dialogue, since what is at issue is a question of emphasis that does not imply hurling anathemas at the unregenerate.

Of course this does not mean that the historians of the French Revolution are now singing in unison. This they never have done and they probably never will. Beneath the differences of interpretation one can detect a new polarization into what is sometimes called the "old" history and the "new." Practitioners of the former believe that what matters is still, as it has always been, the discovery of why things happened as they did. They are convinced that this can only be revealed by investigating the motives of the participants, their perception of the situation in which they found themselves, and the consequences of their attempts to deal with it. The "new" historians, who often borrow their concepts and vocabulary from the social sciences, are more concerned with what the University of California Press recently defined as "innovative explorations of the symbolic constructions of reality." Such explorations attempt to interpret the problems, aspirations, and conflicts of the men and women of the past as having symbolic meanings. History is not so much about events and policies as about the perceptions of our own times. With the help of sociological and psychoanalytical concepts that were not available to the people being studied, the historian can interpret their actions in ways meaningful to the present, of which the historical actors themselves may have been unaware. Each approach has its merits and its dangers.

This seems to me to put the matter quite well; of course, now that we have all read Freud we can hardly ignore the idea that people may have had unconscious motives or neurotic drives, but it is just as obvious that no one who participated in the French Revolution could possibly have thought in those terms. Since psychoanalysis has indeed penetrated everywhere and some understanding of it is a base requirement for any educated person today, our new history writing must reflect that. Whether psychoanalysis explains everything about a great historical event is quite another matter, but there is no way to judge that without a close look at a given text. The long soft shadows of Marx and Freud will be with us some time yet. The longer and deeper shadows of Plato and Einstein will also, and that is why a certain sophistication is a necessity before writing either old or new history.

But, it seems, the new revisionism is sometimes neither politics nor psychoanalysis. In the *New York Times Book Review* for May 15, 1988, Richard Slotkin, writing about Francis Jennings's *Empire of Fortune: Crowns, Colonies, and Tribes in the Seven Years War in America,* says:

> The publication of Francis Jennings's "Empire of Fortune" marks the completion of a major revisionist study of American colonial history. It is an important book, and like all good revisionist history it should stir some useful controversies—although it appears at a time when prominent historians seem to be demanding a restoration of faith in the old verities and a return to canonical methods.
>
> It would be a shame if this back-to-basics movement succeeded, because revisionist readings of the past are what keep a sense of history alive and functioning. The last 15 years of writing in American history have been so extraordinarily productive and exciting, precisely because the old subject matters have been looked at from the new perspectives of social, economic and cultural history. These new fields have added to the historian's repertory of tools and methods, developed new sources and new ways of reading them, and restored to consciousness the historical experiences of groups—peasants and farmers, blue-collar workers, women and minority groups— that were invisible in the account of canonical historians.

If revisionist history has had one glaring weakness, it is that it has been too analytical and has failed to organize its insights into a new, and better, historical narrative. But Mr. Jennings is both a narrative and an analytical historian. His study of colonial politics is enriched by a sophisticated reading of colonial cultures and of the cultures of the Indians among whom the colonists lived. But he moves beyond cultural analysis to tell the story of how these cultures interacted with and affected each other's development.

From all this, the outsider is likely to conclude that in the past twenty years or so there has been great turmoil in history writing but that at the end of the eighties there seems to be a discernible trend toward the traditional methodology enriched with a deeper understanding of the importance of some considerations that historians used to leave out. That seems all to the good. It also means that anybody writing history today has to know more than ever.

So where does all this get us? At this point, the student of writing should see that, although they share some characteristics, history writing requires greater skill than biography writing. The range of writing ability among historiographers is very wide, but generally the worst published history is still a cut above the worst published biography. History at its best is probably above the abilities of most writers, and yet if a writer does have the talent it can take him far.

My advice to an aspiring historian is to try a small project. Since the research and assembling of a mass of data is the first requirement of the historian, a novice is wise to choose some narrow and easily defined subject—perhaps a family history, the story of a single organization like a church or a business company, or the history of a small town—that is entirely manageable and capable of being exhaustively researched. Only by trying to pull that data together into a coherent work will an aspiring writer find out whether or not he has the makings of a historian.

Anyone seriously thinking of a career as a historian or as a history writer should read *Reflections on History and Historians* by Theodore S. Hamerow. The chapter titles are as follows: Chapter I—The Crisis in History; Chapter II—The Professionalization of Historical Learning; Chapter III—Becoming a Historian; Chapter IV—History as a Way of Life; Chapter V—The New History and the Old; and Chapter VI—What Is the Use of History? The author is unusually frank, and since he is a professional his views should be trustworthy. In any case, his book is easy and quick to read because he is an almost perfect example of the topic-sentence writer. Each paragraph opens with a statement, and the rest of that paragraph then explains, justifies, or amplifies that topic sentence; thus the impatient reader can easily skim the book by reading nothing but the first line of each paragraph, and by reading only the paragraphs whose topic sentences are interesting. If the first sentence is a grabber— "For most faculty members a total commitment to the academic way of life, with its intermingling of private and professional experiences, is not a heavy burden"—then you can read the whole paragraph and find out why he does not think that such total commitment is stifling, restrictive, and debilitating as most people might think. If the sentence doesn't interest you—"The information obtained by Ladd and Lipset from more than 60,000 professors in nearly 30 disciplines reveal that political scientists are indeed not atypical"—then move on. Editors have to learn this kind of thing for survival, but students can use such tricks to good effect as well. And I am not being flip. I know enough about this book to know that my recommendation is sound, but I myself have no intention of becoming a historian, so while much of what is in this book is really not for me, that doesn't mean that it isn't for you. Hamerow's writing should intimidate no one, since it is standard academic fare, but I do hope that the readers of this book will learn to stay away from such stuff. If you want to say "typical" just say "typical" and don't say "not atypical."

In any case I remain an outsider in the matter of writing history, and so it seems best to allow a historian to have the last word on the subject. Here is a recent letter to the *New York Times* on January 20, 1988, by Barbara J. Field, professor of history at Columbia University, with which I heartily concur:

We need reminding periodically that history belongs not to professional historians but to those who live it: that is, to the human race as a whole. I am sorry, however, that the discussion (letters, Jan. 3 and 13) should be reduced to such superficial terms: Historians cannot write anymore. Writing about kings and battles is elitist. Studies of gender and race ought to (or, depending on your camp, ought not to) replace studies of major episodes in diplomacy and international relations, Presidential administrations, the development of law under the Constitution and other standard topics.

Let me start with "historians cannot write anymore." It is true that most historians are not great writers. But then, most writers are not great writers; only a few are. No one any longer reads the work of mediocre contemporaries of Herodotus, Tacitus or Michelet. Fifty years from now, no one will read today's mediocrities either. But people will read, to give a few examples, Eric J. Hobsbawn, C. Vann Woodward, Eugene D. Genovese, Willie Lee Rose and John Hope Franklin—probably complaining all the while that no one writes as well as they did, or manages as they did to combine profound analysis with telling an engaging story. I venture to predict that future generations will find the last 50 years or so more remarkable for the number of first-rate historians whose work will have endured than for the number of mediocrities whose work will have passed away. Just considering those writing in English, ours may appear as a golden age of historians.

Because I am a professional historian, I am not free, as future generations will be, to read only today's best. I have to keep up with the literature. Therefore I, too, complain about historians who cannot write and spend a good deal of my time training the next generation to write better. But I would be a poor historian if I pretended that mediocrity was the peculiar property of the so-called new history. Alas, it is an integral part of the human condition.

As to elitism: Elitism does not inhere in subject matter, but in approach. An elitist may write about ordinary people, just as a democrat may write about kings and generals. The historian whose work deserves to last is the one whose agenda, whatever the topic of study, is the highest possible development of humanity's potential; not one part of humanity, but the whole of it. Such an agenda may animate the study of a general or the study of a slave. It may well be rooted in a view of what best promotes human development that not everyone shares: what a bore, if we all did. We do not learn only from those we agree with. A conservative, a Marxist, a feminist and a Christian fundamentalist may all concern themselves with questions that should matter to everyone. The largeness of the vision, not the unanimity of its reception, is what counts.

Poor writing and trivial thinking among professional historians is a bad sign for our society—as is the same malady among leaders in business and government and among professionals in the mass media—and we need to think deeply about what it portends. But that means casting off illusions about golden ages that are golden only because they have passed. And it means recognizing that not what we study, but what we ask, will determine the quality of our thought.

Writing
TO
TELL A STORY

FICTION

FICTION IS ART. This book is about craft and competence. For that reason I shall confine my remarks to what the student of writing ought to know about how to become competent at fiction from the point of view of the publisher. If I were to use our *good, better, best* system with examples I should be acting as a literary critic, and I have no intention of doing that. For one thing, what pleases a publisher and what excites a critic are two entirely different things, and for another, literary critics are notorious for their lack of unanimity. In any case, the student wants to know how to get published and how to learn to become a good writer of fiction, and on that subject I can speak from a publisher's point of view.

In the first place, since fiction is art, it is important to remember that art does not spring full grown from the brow. Young editors at publishing houses are astonished to find that although aspiring painters, for example, would never expect an art gallery to mount an exhibition of their first pictures, nonetheless aspiring novelists never cease to expect their first novel to be given serious consideration for publication. But learning to write a novel is at least as hard as learning, say, to fly a plane, or to handle a ship, or to run a printing press. A student in any of those fields takes completely for granted that a long apprenticeship is an absolutely necessary requirement before he will be allowed to take the controls. The same assumption should be made by the student who wishes to become a novelist. On the other hand, everybody in publishing is also aware of novelists who come out of nowhere, are turned down all over the place, and yet find a publisher and achieve fame. Nevertheless, readers of this book must understand that these cases do not prove that anyone can write a novel and get rich and famous. Quite the contrary. Those cases are sports—one-in-a-thousand shots that are more to be compared to a winning lottery ticket than the reward of genius and hard work. The great majority of novels are written by conscientious professionals who have usually learned what they know the hard way, by practicing it until they were successful at it. Most novelists regard what they do as their life as well as their livelihood and have not come to it casually or without plenty of testing and training. For that reason I urge the would-be fiction writer to think of writing as no different from any other profession; the course ahead is just as long and just as full of plain hard work.

It is true that art is sometimes produced by people with no training, but it is also true that the great majority of serious artists in any field have first learned their craft and done their apprenticeships. Conversely, people with no natural talent for art have sometimes trained themselves for years to learn their craft but still have not produced art—for some people no amount of practice is going to get them to the point of producing publishable work.

Some unpublished authors cannot understand why all their effort does not pay off when they see other people getting published who haven't done anything like a comparable amount of work. There is nothing to tell these people but that talent is unevenly distributed in any population, and some people were just born with more talent than others. Nevertheless, most published writers are professionals, and the only way to become a professional is through training, practice, and hard work.

At this point, the student should consider what goes on in an editor's head when he is considering a new piece of work for publication. What does an editor want?

Well, first of all, an editor wants to keep his job. Of course he would love to be a discoverer of new talent, and it is pleasant to become known as someone who handles very successful books; but to keep his job he must handle books that, on balance, make money. No editor whose books consistently lose money will ever keep a job for very long. Everybody in publishing knows that editors, like the publishing houses they work for, only stay in business by making a profit. So editors look for money-makers. The question then becomes, what makes money?

At this point the writer must face the simple realities of writing and publishing, which, while not complicated, are nonetheless inescapable. A trade book (i.e., not a book that is required to be bought, such as the text for a college course) is merely an object offered for sale by a publisher. Nothing more and nothing less. The purchase of a book is a free choice made by a buyer who could just as well have spent the money on something else. Books can be left lying in the bookstore while the same money pays for a meal in a restaurant, a couple of movie tickets, the rental of a movie for the home VCR, or dozens of other discretionary items, including a flag to put up in front of the house on the Fourth of July. In short, books are in competition with an almost unimaginable number of other possible items that may strike the fancy of a buyer. With so many other attractive things around to spend money on, what can a book offer that is superior? Well, what indeed?

The answer, of course, is that books can and do offer whole worlds apart, powerful and moving stories, insight into the depths of human character, enthralling mysteries to be solved, and a fresh understanding of ourselves and the world around us. No book offers all of these things, but if it offers any one of them in abundance it may attract enough buyers to make both the author and the publisher some money. The trade-book business is a *business,* not a philanthropy and not an educational endeavor. Trade books sell and the business thrives if and only if people feel that they got their money's worth from buying and reading a book.

It may be observed in passing that books as objects do have some purely technical advantages over other purchases that could have been made with the same money. It takes longer to read a book than to see a movie; a book is tangible while a movie is only a puff of smoke. When you have finished reading a book it is still there, ready to be shelved, lent to a friend, or given to someone else; a restaurant meal leaves nothing but indigestion. A lovely concert vanishes into an insubstantial memory, but a book can be reopened and reread. In short, a book is a durable object, and that very consideration makes many people choose books over less lasting offerings. But even when we grant that all the above is true, the content of the book also has to offer something to make it attractive enough to be worth the fancy price that is asked for it.

What, then, is an editor looking for when he reads a fiction manuscript? He is looking for something *attractive.* And what attracts? Well, most of all, a good story. *Tell me a story* is something that parents hear from children who are still very young. *Let me tell you a story* is a phrase that will stop almost anyone and immediately arrest his attention. So underneath almost all fiction there lies a story, however cleverly it may be concealed. The events of the story may be entirely banal and the true story nothing but layers of information peeled off, one by one, to reveal bits of the inner core, until it lies there in all its triviality, but even that in its way is a story. Writing does not reward randomness. Disjointed bits will not hold a reader. Dadaism and abstract expressionism don't work well with words. Words strung together must have a coherent meaning or they are not communication and the reader will leave them in frustration. Words must communicate ideas that they represent and must do so in an understandable manner, or they aren't even considered writing at all. What holds words together is a line of thought, discernible to the reader as a line. It can be pretty obscure, but if there is a thread to follow, readers will persevere. We call that line a story, and that is the first thing an editor looks for.

The second thing an editor looks for is readability. Does this author draw you into his story in a sort of irresistible way and hook you into what he is saying? Do the words flow in such a way that your mind concentrates on what is being said and not on how it is being said? Are you even aware you are reading? If you *are* aware, that is a bad sign. If the story becomes so interesting that you are really not aware that you are reading, that is a wonderful sign. So the editor asks, does it flow? Does it get to me right away? Does it suck me in in spite of myself? If the answer is yes, then he may be in the hands of a writer.

Then the editor asks more questions. Who are the characters? Can I identify with them? Do they seem real and alive? Can I recognize traits in them that touch me? Do I care about them? When I read along, are my emotions engaged? If he answers yes to all these questions, he knows that he has something in his hands that can possibly be turned into money. If the answer is no, he will write a short report and the manuscript will go back from whence it came.

But when an editor gets a manuscript that he loves reading, that moves him, and that he thinks has great possibilities, he then turns his inquiries from the manuscript to its author. Is he someone young and promising, so that a publication of this book may well be the start of a long and fruitful collaboration, or is he someone from whom nothing more can be expected? The answer counts a lot. Is the author someone with whom he can work? If the answer is no—perhaps the author is an arrogant and presumptuous type who doesn't want to change a word of his precious book on anyone's account—then that is a bad sign. If the author is willing to listen to and take suggestions seriously, that is a good sign. So on one side or the other of the balance goes the editor's appraisal of the author.

The editor also tries to place the manuscript in the context of past and current fiction. What is this book like? The work of most authors reflects to some degree the concerns and styles of what he has read, so the editor looks for parallels between the manuscript at hand and already published and well-known fiction. Is this work like that of the young Hemingway? Does it read like John Cheever or perhaps John Rechey? Is it as convoluted as Faulkner or as plain as Stephen Crane? How does it compare to the thousands of books currently being offered to readers? Is it essentially literary in its appeal or less highbrow? What sense can be made of this manuscript by likening it to other well-known work? Can it be described in a handy shorthand, by a catch-phrase, for example? How could the publishing house promote it? What is there about it that might make it stand out?

When all of these questions have been answered to the editor's satisfaction, then he has to think of the serious questions that lie behind all others: Can this book make its own way? Can this author, either with this book or with another, produce a best-seller? These two questions drive right to the heart of what publishing is all about, and no writer who wishes to become a professional can afford to ignore their importance, and so we must examine each one in some detail.

Most books, to be successful, do have to make their own way. Amateurs and outsiders assume that if a publisher spends a lot of money on advertising and promotion then a book will sell, and so many authors blame their publisher's lack of effort when their books don't make it big. But people outside of publishing should understand that advertising cannot and does not sell books. Advertising by publishers is largely ineffectual because, first, even when the publisher spends what is by his standards a huge sum of money it is still peanuts in the advertising business as a whole, and, second, book advertising is mostly aimed at booksellers, not consumers.

These propositions are central to basic problems of publishing. If a big publisher announces that a book that it expects to become a best-seller will have "major national advertising" or some such phrase, it means that it will spend $100,000 or even perhaps $150,000 to promote the book. And what does that buy? As of the middle of 1989, a full-page ad in the *New York Times Book Review* cost $14,-565. A very common size ad known as a 75 × 2, which is two columns wide and seventy-five agate lines deep (about 5¼ inches), in the daily *New York Times* costs $3415; in *The Chicago Tribune,* $1932; in the *Los Angeles Times,* $3697; and in the daily *Providence Journal,* $1132. It is easy to see that if the publisher has taken some advance space in *Publishers Weekly* at $3030 a page, in *Library Journal* at $2365 a page, and in a few other trade papers his entire budget will be used up in a matter of a few days. Amounting to only one tenth of the ad budget for a movie, say, which is typically $1 million or $1.5 million, the money publishing houses spend on promotion is a mere teaspoonful in the vast lake of American advertising and cannot be enough to affect the buying choices of very many people.

But publishers spend that money not to sell you books, but to make sure that the book trade has books to sell you. That is, a publisher announces a big campaign to convince bookstores that it thinks it has a big book, is going to back it with money, and "create demand." Bookstores will always order books that publishers are backing with big campaigns because, although they are as cynical as everybody else about the effectiveness of advertising, they would rather have advertised books around than ones that don't have the publisher's support.

Students at this point must remember some basic truths about bookselling. As anyone who has ever worked in a bookstore knows, nonfiction is mostly bought by men while

80 percent of fiction is purchased by women. Bookstore people also know that, although there are exceptions, the majority of women do not know what they want when they enter a bookstore, so they tend to buy what is already in the store and on display. If a sign on a big stack of a book right in the front of the store proclaims that the book is a big best-seller, then that book has a much better chance than most of attracting purchasers. Bookstores thus largely sell what they have, and that is why a publisher goes to so much trouble to make sure stores stock the books it is pushing. Stores usually choose what to take by the "level of support"—the advertising budget—the publisher announces it will give a book. The best-seller syndrome thus feeds on itself.

Does everybody in publishing know this? Indeed they do. Is this a scandal? No, because everybody also knows that advertising doesn't sell unknown books anyway. It sells what are called brand name books—books that are written by authors whose work is recognized as a genre in itself. In our time that means a new book by Stephen King, Sidney Sheldon, or James A. Michener, but every age has its own favorites.

So, then, what does sell books? Word of mouth is far and away the most effective way that books are sold, but it is also the surest means of killing sales of an unpopular book. The only way a publisher can get a favorable word-of-mouth campaign started is to enthuse a few influential people. That is why, especially for books such as first novels, getting copies into the hands of people who will probably like the book is so important. Thus publishers send out lots of galleys for advance quotes, ship generous numbers of copies to reviewers, and wait anxiously for positive reviews.

A review is very much like a friend who has read the book: the opinion is taken seriously by people who might make readers. But notice that people who like the book and reviewers who write good reviews are both influenced by the book itself, not by anything the publisher has to say about it. Thus it is the author and the author's writing that either make friends or fail to do so. Because publishers know all this as well as anyone, they habitually spend only modest sums on promoting first novels, preferring to wait and see if a book can make any friends on its own before committing themselves to any large expenditure.

At this point my readers are likely to be saying to themselves, well, then, if print advertising doesn't sell books, does television exposure? The answer to that is yes it does, but that authors who get television exposure are almost all writers of a nonfiction book. The television interviewer needs to have something to talk about—a hook. That hook is the subject of the book at hand—a new diet, the opening up of a political scandal, the life of a celebrity, or even the author's own adventures, something, anything, to hang the interview on.

Novels, especially first novels, don't really have a hook. If a new author makes a huge success, then that in itself can be the hook, but the novel itself can almost never serve as the hook. It is true that an obscure book can be lifted to bestsellerdom by a television interview, but such a book will almost always be nonfiction and usually a self-help book at that. It is also true that famous best-selling fiction authors get on television, but that is because by then they are interesting to television because of their fame and their status, not because of their new book. Notice that during such an interview everybody talks about everything *but* what is in the new book.

Thinking about all this must be depressing to the would-be novelist, but what may sustain him, as it does his publisher, is the knowledge that someday, perhaps, he too may become rich and famous. Rich? Yes, it is possible, and to that idea we now turn.

In the last forty years publishing has grown from a modest business into a big business, and nothing has affected its metamorphosis as profoundly as the growth of the best-seller syndrome. As the publishing business grew, it developed into a few dominant organizations. On the bookselling side, the explosive growth of chain bookstores enabled them to order books by the thousands and even tens of thousands, which gave them a great deal of power in the publishing world. Only publishing units as big and as important as the chains could match their influence, so the superpublisher developed simultaneously. We now have about a dozen major publishing groups that dominate the whole book trade, and undoubtedly these organizations are big business. There is also no question but that to continue to be big and profitable, they need big books. Thus the large publishers actively seek out and compete for best-sellers; they actually *need* best-sellers to sustain their level of business. This fact has practical consequences for authors: since big publishers are constantly on the lookout for new talent, an author who writes a best-seller can indeed become rich.

The fiction writer, especially the unpublished fiction writer, often views big publishers as monolithic and inscrutable, a sort of giant beast to be approached with caution and with the sure knowledge that its actions will always be inscrutable and irrational. If that writer knows that in the furthest reaches of the mind of each person he talks to at a big publishing house there lies only one question—can this writer become a best-seller for us?—then his sense of the publisher's irrationality will disappear. The only underlying motive any employee of a big publishing house has is his drive toward getting and keeping best-sellers. A promising young author will be eagerly taken on, nursed through hundreds of tiny problems, cosseted, cajoled, and sustained through all the pains of publication if—and only if—his editors believe that, however difficult or tempermental he is, he may someday become their own bread and butter. A truly big best-seller can establish a publishing career and ensure a company many months' worth of satisfactory balance sheets. Every employee of a big publishing house knows that *without* best-sellers the house could not operate, and that knowledge colors every action taken and every choice made.

Since it takes time for an author to establish a good reputation and since almost no best-seller is written by a first-time author, the big publishing houses are all constantly on the lookout for new talent. They have to publish, say, twenty first novelists in order to find one who will go on to the big time. The ratio is actually worse than that, I think, but I haven't made a statistical study of it. In any case, the fact is that very, very few first novelists actually go on to make it big.

The point is that the big houses *are* willing to take risks. They *have* to take risks or they will never find their future best-selling writers. They have to let their young editors develop their own writers because editors need practice as much as anyone else in order to become fully professional. So, yes, lots of first novels are published. The real problem is not that the young author cannot find a publisher, but that generally publishers are constantly putting out completely untried stuff in the hope that it will catch on by itself.

It is unfortunate but true that for a publisher the only way to do market research is to publish a book and find out if it has a market. But it is actually not very expensive to publish and find that the market for a book is quite small, so it is better to have tried it than to have failed to take the risk. Since it does happen that every so often one of these obscure books breaks out all on its own and becomes big, the large houses feel that publishing the books that young editors really feel enthusiastic about is well worthwhile. After all, the losses taken on books that don't pay their own way are more than offset by the profits from the best-sellers. So, yes, there is room in this relentless quest for money not only for newcomers but for "literary" newcomers.

In nonfiction an editor and publisher always have a subject to deal with and so there is usually a well-defined group to whom the book may be sold. Since works of fiction have no such discernible group to aim at, publishers have to rely on reviews to break novels, especially first novels, out of the pack. To interest potential reviewers, they must depend upon their reputation for producing good books, so they go to considerable lengths to acquire and maintain that good reputation. But the opposite situation also exists: some houses are known for putting out nothing but irredeemable junk, so an author whose work bears the imprint of such a house cannot expect to be noticed, no matter what he has written.

Consider the case of, say, Farrar, Straus & Giroux, Inc., which has a well-deserved reputation for producing high-quality literature. If it sends a reviewer a first novel, its reputation is such that the reviewer will almost certainly look at it twice. The difference in the reception given books published by Farrar, Straus, for example, and those churned out by a low-level publisher is worth a lot of money. Sophisticated publishing houses know that, and so the good ones make a point of publishing not only a lot of new novels but also strictly "literary" books that, although they may lose money, will enhance their standing as publishers of quality books. So, paradoxically, the relentless drive for the big buck leads in the end to some quite good literary publishing. That conclusion may seem irrational—and certainly a great many people who consider themselves "literary" disagree with it—but any dispassionate analysis of the actual lists of the dozen biggest publishers will confirm it.

So where does all this leave the unpublished writer? He should now see that publishing is big, complicated, and in some respects inscrutable, but that the big houses are surprisingly open to new talent, and that beyond them are hundreds of smaller publishers who are also always on the lookout for talent. All the writer needs to do is to train himself to become professional, learn his craft, and then persist.

JOURNALISM

JOURNALISM IS THE WRITING AND PUBLISHING of news for print and electronic media. A vast field, it includes everything from our great metropolitan daily newspapers to small regional weeklies, from magazines with circulations of one million copies a week to tiny specialist quarterlies, from broadcasts of news on television by world-famous figures to family announcements on regional foreign-language access channels and local radio. Its subjects can be anything from the events of the day to background features, interviews, panel discussions or analyses of current events. Journalism uses a huge amount of material on a daily basis and is therefore a natural place for a writer to break into print; indeed many of our most famous writers have started their careers in journalism. Any aspiring writer, then, must consider journalism as a potential place to begin.

First, a caveat: the reader of this book must remember that I have spent my working lifetime in the book business and so have written this book strictly from the point of view of the would-be book writer. Although I do not feel qualified to write much about journalism per se, I do know about journalism in relation to the book business, and it is that uneasy link that we will be thinking about.

There are profound differences in basic attitudes about writing in the two worlds of journalism and book publishing. We shall have a look at these differences so that we can see the *distance* between the two worlds.

In the first place, there is in the two worlds a profound difference in an editor's attitude toward copy. Anyone writing for a newspaper or magazine will soon discover that a writer's copy has no sacred standing with editors there. Magazines and papers have rewrite editors who feel entirely free to take the reporter's copy and reshape it, edit it, cut it, or adapt it as they see fit. The original writer does not get the luxury of being consulted as to whether he likes what happens to his copy. What he turns in is regarded as a sort of raw material to be shaped to the needs of the publication. Of course it varies tremendously from one publication to another, but this does not change the fact that basic attitudes are very different. Even the most respected literary monthly magazines will expect a level of editorial control and involvement that seems startling to a writer accustomed to book editors. Almost all journalism is a continuing activity, and it is the identity and character of the paper or journal over time that matters, not any given writer. Writers are used to maintain the publication as it is regularly published and to keep it within its readers' established and well-defined expectations. The editor, then, is the important shaper of the character of his publication as day after day or month after month he brings his readers a product which reflects not his writers but himself. Several magazine editors have become famous and are completely identified with their publications: Harold W. Ross at *The New Yorker,* Henry R. Luce at *Time,* and Tina Brown at *Vanity Fair.* Newspapers, naturally, are much more diverse and complex, but they also establish a character that is not dependent upon the writing of any one reporter or commentator. What appears in any paper or magazine is expected to contribute to the editor's controlling view of what that publication is, and what the writer produces must be shaped to that vision.

In the world of books the situation is almost exactly re-

versed. Each writer is unique and is not held up or surrounded by the works of other writers. Quite the contrary:
each writer must stand alone and offer his book to a public
that will either buy it or not. The audience for each book is
as unique as the book itself. The buyer is the actual reader,
not an editor who is going to publish the work whether or
not a reader wants it. Thus the book editor is inclined to
regard the writer's work as indeed being close to finished.
In addition, a book editor would almost never have the time
to work with a writer on a sentence-by-sentence basis, so
book people become used to either taking on a writer or
rejecting him. If they reject his book, even though it may
have had some good things in it, they often do so precisely
because the task of working with the writer and making
him rewrite this bit, add to that bit, cut here, patch there,
and reshape the entirety is far too tedious and time consum-
ing an undertaking. Unless the flaws in a manuscript are
pretty simple to fix and can be done by the writer with only
basic guidance from the editor, the manuscript will be
passed over entirely. Thus those manuscripts that do get
accepted tend to be pretty close to as good as the editor
thinks those particular writers can make them; he most
definitely does not want to mess around with them. Clearly
there are always exceptions, but the exceptions do not
change the basic differences in the views of editors in journalism and those in the book business.

In the next place, the worlds of journalism and of books
also have profoundly different attitudes about time and how
it is handled. A journalist has to learn to deal with daily
deadlines. He has to become accustomed to knocking out
copy, perfect or not, in order to file his story within his
deadline. This, as everyone knows, makes daily journalism
a high-pressure business, and the pressure really isn't completely alleviated when the writer has a somewhat longer
deadline, as he would for a background piece for a paper, a
report for a weekly, or an article in a monthly. The deadline
is always there, and it is a real deadline: if it is missed the

piece does not run at all. This has some not-so-obvious consequences: once the piece is written and filed it cannot be
changed (at least not by the writer), and so the writer immediately puts it out of his mind in order to prepare for the
next deadline; it also means that yesterday's journalism is
as dead and gone for the reader as it is for the writer. The
ephemeral nature of the journalist's efforts and the endur-
ance of a book editor's work produce very different attitudes
in the people involved, but perhaps a story will illustrate it
best.

When I had just started my own publishing company and
was very innocent, I was also quite short of cash, so I accepted with pleasure an invitation from a very well known
journalist to stay with him when I took a trip to London. He
had built a considerable reputation as a foreign correspon-
dent in Europe during World War II and was very much the
seasoned professional. After dinner at his house one night,
the phone rang: something sensational had just happened—
the Russians, it was said, had just put a satellite in orbit
around the earth. It seemed an impossible and mind-bend-
ing idea, but he learned that to find out anything more
about it we would have to read the first copies of *The Daily
Worker*, a Communist mouthpiece, that would soon be roll-
ing off the presses in Fleet Street. Hardly anybody except
the few faithful read that paper, so, in order to give the
circulation of the *Worker* as much of a boost as they could,
the Russian information people on occasion gave it a scoop.
Come on, he said, let's go.

We hopped in his car, drove down to the plant in Fleet
Street, and, sure enough, were there when the first copies
came out. The *Worker* did indeed carry a big story about the
Russians' satellite, called Sputnik, and it also gave a few
details about the whole thing that had not been known
before. We rushed to his office, where he made a few calls,
taking notes as he talked, then knocked out a story on his
old typewriter, and finally read the story over the phone to
the international operator and that was that. As soon as he

hung up the phone, he expressed satisfaction with a job well done and suggested that we repair to the journalists' local all-night pub for a nightcap, which we did. The entire episode had taken little more than an hour.

The whole thing amazed me. As soon as the story was filed he had no further interest in it, and we didn't talk about it any more that night or the next day either. Once his story was filed, his mind simply turned off. In contrast, I never turned off or stopped thinking about what I was doing. Book writers are mostly the same: they simply *are* book writers, so the idea of cutting all that out of their consciousness at any moment and thinking of something else would have seemed absurd. It seemed as if the people involved in books were *being* something while journalists were *doing* something. In other words, journalism is a job while book writing is a condition of life.

In journalism, then, time is segmented, immediate, pressing, and then gone, while with books time is something that flows along as a continuum. You insert your work into the flow as best you can, let it go when it is ready, and hope that it becomes a part of the cultural stream, flowing on and on to become one with the great sea in which we all swim. Whether the work becomes part of the living stream at any specific point of time is a matter of secondary importance to the attempt to make it count, to have it be important and noticed and bought and read. That it does not get thrown out with the fish bones in yesterday's paper but strives to become part of the larger culture in a more or less permanent way is what counts.

Attitudes about time, then, in ways both obvious and subtle are very different indeed in the two worlds, and the writer working in one or the other will be rewarded by keeping that in mind.

As an aside to our consideration of how time works differently in the two worlds, let me point out why the great events that often constitute the focus of journalism's finest achievements often turn out to be marginal when they become the subject of books. I learned that lesson during and after the Hungarian Revolution of 1956—a popular revolt against the Russian-backed Communist regime that at first aroused wild hopes and then was crushed by Russian tanks, creating a flood of refugees to America and lasting impressions of youths thirsty for freedom using hardly more than stones to attack the armor arrayed against them. The news magazines used such arresting images for their covers, television—still crude—showed what pictures it could get, and the papers were full of news of the revolt for weeks on end.

Since the Hungarians' futile efforts touched a great many people very deeply, we (the staff of my publishing house and I) thought that a big book about it, quickly done, would be a great seller. We did one, but it proved a disappointment. We were very surprised. Why shouldn't people want a book on the great subject of the day?

After we tried a few more books like it, we realized the answer: anything that is very closely covered by the news media over a period of days and weeks (in our own time think of the Challenger disaster) is pretty well done for. The news media, especially, of course, the great newspapers and the news magazines, are now so thorough in their coverage of a big event that by the time a book comes out people feel that they already know all that they want to about it. Unless a book contains revelations that were never covered by the media, the story has already been told and the only interest is a historical one. Book writers and publishers cannot and should not try to do what news people do faster and better. Books are not for news. Books are for the record.

Another problem with journalism is bias, or perhaps more properly, the point of view of the writer. As we have seen in the section on writing history, an implicit understanding between the writer and the reader of history is that the writer is impartial, objective, and interested only in telling his story as well as possible without distorting it through some ideological lens. To this day if a historian is known as a purely Marxist historian or a feminist historian, whatever he writes will be read in light of that bias. Today, ideological journals, newspapers, and newscasts are also taken with a grain of salt but it was not always so. We also cannot assume that bias is always obvious or that the modern reader is alert to signs of it.

Looking at our great newspapers today it is hard to remember that the independent and unbiased newspaper we have come to expect is a very recent development. Historically, practically all papers were the mouthpiece of an interest group, a religion, or a political party. There were a lot of papers and there was plenty of competition for readers as well.

The great flowering of American print journalism was from the Civil War until the Depression. In the 1920s, for example, New York had something like twenty daily papers, including the *Sun,* the *Times,* the *Herald,* the *World,* the *Daily News,* the *Post,* and the Brooklyn *Eagle.* Eventually the *Herald* became the *Herald Tribune,* and the *Journal* became the *Journal American* until, as a result of the long period of consolidation that followed World War II and the growth of television, they merged and then died. In addition, the immigrants flooding the streets read their news in such ethnic papers as *La Prensa, El Progresso,* and the *Jewish Daily Forward,* or in foreign-language papers printed in Greek, Chinese, Hebrew, or other languages.

What all this meant was that when one read a paper one would know ahead of time that when the paper ran an article about matters that touched upon its sponsorship it would reflect the opinions and position of that sponsorship. For instance, the *New York Herald Tribune,* which, in its day, was a very well respected paper, was the voice of the liberal wing of the Republican party, and thus when reporting on American politics it would reflect that point of view. Its readers were expected to know where the *Trib* stood just as modern-day readers of *The Economist* are expected to know that its point of view is Tory but not necessarily Thatcherite.

In all cases, however, the reader expected that the paper, when it was not writing about something of interest to its sponsorship, would be entirely fair-minded. That is, when the *Trib* reported on, say, a crime in the Irish slums it just gave the facts and did not take the occasion to write a sermon on American immigration policies as seen from a nativist and establishment point of view. In the *Trib* the reader could assume that simple news stories were just that. In the papers owned by William Randolph Hearst, on the other hand, one could not be so sure. The voice of the far right wing of the Republican party, his papers might well use a crime in the Irish slums as an occasion to make a political point. As a result, the Hearst papers never earned the respect of a well-educated public while the *Trib* did.

The establishment of completely independent papers and unbiased news columns is in fact a rather recent development in American journalism. Up until the Great Depression virtually all papers and most magazines were written from a distinct point of view. The formation and expansion of the Associated Press and other generalized news agencies served the cause of even-handedness: because they supplied news items to papers of every position, their own copy had to be neutral. In addition, the *New York Times* over many years was a champion of objectivity in its news columns. Nonetheless only in the 1930s did individual journalists begin to insist upon their intellectual independence and lack of inherent bias.

I have not seen much in the way of studies of all this, although they must exist, but my impression is that during the 1930s the opinions of the newspaper owners, who were almost to a man bitterly against Roosevelt, were deeply opposed by most of the people who worked and wrote for them. Thus in the 1930s and certainly through the two Eisenhower-Stevenson campaigns, the newspaper owners were for one candidate while the writers were for the other, a situation that still holds today. The only lasting agreement between them was that editorial columns would reflect the owners' opinions while the news columns were to be *unbiased* and completely objective. This had been the claim of the *New York Times* for many years.

Since objective reporters helped produce a much better newspaper and one that people were more willing to trust to tell them the truth, those papers that became known for their independent and unbiased news columns prospered, while the mouthpieces of specific points of view started to languish. As a result, our great papers today are all published with the understanding that news columns are written without bias while editorial columns are clearly labeled as such. Even as partisan a set of owners as those of the *Wall Street Journal* expect their reporters to be of an independent mind and to give, for example, equal space to the views of opposing political campaigns.

A look at the present position of the *Christian Science Monitor* is quite instructive. Established, like so many other papers, as the organ of a religious sect and one that holds beliefs that the vast majority of citizens would take to be eccentric (a preference for spiritual over "material" methods of healing), the paper nevertheless holds an almost unique place of trust in the minds of serious readers and especially other members of the journalistic profession. Why is this? The answer is that in fields where the tenets of the religion have no say one way or the other—and these fields include politics, foreign affairs, economics, and the general course of current world events—the paper's editors and writers write completely objectively. The paper's religious columns are clearly labeled as such.

The big papers like the *Washington Post* and the *New York Times* in dealing with the government, for example, find themselves to some degree the captive of the administration then in power. What the White House spokesman says is news, and even if what he says is a lie, it must be reported. One need only think of the endless duplicities that issued from Lyndon Johnson's White House and later from Richard Nixon's to bring the problem into focus. A newspaper's White House reporter may know very well that today's story of the body count from Vietnam is a sham, but he is still obliged to report not only the spokesman's figures but his statement that those figures encouraged the president in his belief that the light at the end of the tunnel was not far away. That is what the man said, and that is what must be reported because what the White House says on any given day constitutes the news of the day. The *Monitor,* much less in the pocket of the daily process and not feeling the need to be the newspaper of record, can choose not to run a story if the editors think it is based on obvious White House propaganda. Its ability to *distance* itself from daily events makes what the *Christian Science Monitor* does report all the more noteworthy. The paradox, then, is that the great dailies whose owners want to be absolutely independent are in fact obliged to become the mouthpieces for the establishment while the voice of a small sect can be relied upon to take a fearlessly independent look at that same establishment.

It is interesting to note that small religious groups with plenty of money continue to publish today. The Reverend Sun Myung Moon and his Unification Church have put out an expensive giveaway called *Plain Truth,* which for a time appeared in a lot of supermarkets, but apparently it failed to persuade enough people that its contents lived up to its title. L. Ron Hubbard's Church of Scientology is now putting out an expensive slick weekly news magazine called *Freedom;* although it claims to publish *Investigative Reporting in the Public Interest,* it seems to consist almost entirely of shrill articles against the evils of drugs. Neither publication can expect to build up a large readership among those who have no underlying interest in the religious group behind the publication, but both efforts are reminders of how long it takes and how hard it is for a publication with a religious sponsorship to establish a solid reputation.

American magazines of general interest had no discernible bias in the sense we've been discussing, but each did reflect the ideas and interests of its editor. William Dean Howells, first in the *Atlantic Monthly* and later in *Harper's Magazine,* only promoted realism in American literature. George Horace Lorimer of the *Saturday Evening Post* just printed what it pleased him to read, such as stories that shared his simple country ideas and that painted a rosy view of American life and aspirations, and the American public eagerly read what he published. Although S. S. McClure in his own *McClure's Magazine* published most of the great muckraking articles of Lincoln Steffens, Ida Tarbell and Ray Stannard Baker it was probably with an eye more to increasing circulation than to furthering any social agenda.

With the establishment of *Time* and other weekly news magazines, that changed. Anyone who has read any of the numerous memoirs of former writers who worked for Luce will learn about the acute frustration they experienced in his employ. *Time* was just as much one long editorial as any copy of the *Daily Worker,* only *Time* was published with the overt claim of objectivity. Under Luce, the magazine reflected his own reactionary ideas, which he held with the missionary zeal taught to him by his father in China. His writers, who knew they were the best paid in the business and that, by design, were almost all liberal and almost always of a completely different mind. They would file their stories, but the versions that were published would often give almost the exact opposite impression to what the authors intended. It drove them wild but since few could afford to give up the fine pay checks they got, they stayed on, breeding ulcers or becoming future candidates for the ministrations of AA while Luce grimly pursued his agenda. Things have seemed to improve since his death, but to this day most news magazines do not have the reputation for fairness and objectivity that the best newspapers enjoy.

It is ironic and not a little depressing to realize that at just about the time that reporters for most publications were finally independent entities who considered it an almost sacred trust to write without any preconceptions, a new style of journalism began to develop that not only questioned but boldly laid aside the basic idea of the reporter's impartiality. The new attitude has been called The New Journalism or advocacy journalism, and its position has been laid out in *The Art of Writing Nonfiction*, a textbook written by Andre Fontaine and William A. Glavin, Jr. Both men were magazine editors before they joined the faculty of the S. I. Newhouse School of Public Communications at Syracuse University.

According to Fontaine and Glavin, "Interpretive journalism is a process, based on rigorous reportage, that employs the creativity and skills of the fiction writer and presents the judgment of the writer, after he or she has objectively evaluated the facts, of where the truth lies." They also point to the work of Tom Wolfe, Truman Capote, Jimmy Breslin, and Gay Talese as exemplars of the genre, and their book proceeds to show how it is done.

Whatever the merits of the New Journalism may be, and I for one am extremely dubious about them, it is certain that a writer must learn the usual techniques of the objective reporter before he can assume the luxury of ignoring those techniques and their underlying assumptions.

Since the publication of Truman Capote's *In Cold Blood*, whether the nonfiction novel was a legitimate new category of writing has been debated, and the controversy has not yet been resolved and probably never will be. I believe that the form is not and cannot become legitimate. For example, Capote claimed that he did not record his interviews with the two doomed murderers whose story was told in the book because his memory of their conversation was so accurate that it rendered a tape recorder superfluous. That's doubtful. He also maintained that the presence of a tape recorder would have been inhibiting, and in that one would have to concur.

Here we get to a deep problem. Some novelists have an ear for human speech that is so good that when they write dialogue it sounds absolutely convincing. John O'Hara wrote like that. When reading his novels, one could actually hear his characters talk, but he denies having taped actual speech. Like any artist, O'Hara used what he knew to create an illusion of reality so strong that it may be almost more convincing than life itself. Nevertheless a novel by him is a work of art and it is presented as such. Capote, in quoting his murderers is also creating a work of art that seems in a way more real than real, but for him to tell us that his ear is correct is only to convince any knowledgeable observer that he has never read transcripts of how people actually speak. The editorial impulse and drive for meaning is so strong in most listeners that the imperfections caught in an accurate transcript—the pauses, odd unintelligible sounds, elisions, slurring of sounds and words, and sentence fragments—are ignored or not noticed; but for a writer to claim that he only recorded what he heard just as he heard it is as impossible in fact as it is disingenuous in practice. But if that is so, where does it leave Capote's claim that he has told the story exactly as it was? It is truly hard to say, since I am convinced that he did tell the whole story as well as he could without *consciously* introducing a point of view and a judgment—that in fact his *own* performance was in cold blood.

No, I do not advocate the new journalism. The readers of this book should remember, however, that advocacy journalism is a long step beyond standard journalism, which is hard enough to learn in any case.

The would-be journalist has plenty of places where he can start to learn. Most high schools and colleges have student-run papers and magazines. If my own experience is typical, the harried student who finds himself the editor of any one of those publications is only too glad to welcome people who want to write for the publication. Even marginal writers are often accepted if they are enthusiastic and willing to work. That experience gives the young writer what is most needed—practice and more practice.

If the aspiring journalist hasn't done much in school or college, he still might enroll in one of the long-established journalism schools, the oldest of which was established at the University of Wisconsin in 1905, and probably the most famous of which is at Columbia University.

But what about the journalist who wishes to switch over from one world to the other? Do I have any advice for him? Yes, and it is simply that if he ever intends to switch from journalism to books, he should do it while he's young. From what I have seen of journalists, if they stay at it any length of time they have a hard time turning off the habits of mind and the turn of style that makes them good journalists in the first place. Learning how to work within the journalistic style is all to the good, for it has many virtues—as we shall see in more detail when we consider style in a later chapter—but a person who practices it for any length of time tends to adopt it as his very own style, and a more expansive, discursive, and analytical approach becomes difficult if not impossible for him.

To summarize, I'd advise a person who is interested in and has a knack for journalism to try it, but unless he likes it enough to make it his career he should get out of it while still young.

Writing

TO

INSTRUCT
AND
EXPLAIN

HOW-TO-DO-IT BOOKS

WRITING BEGAN AS A MEANS OF STORING DATA and quickly proved to be of immense value in establishing facts and then recording them accurately. We have seen in the foregoing chapters how writing has been used as a store of human memory, first in keeping one's own memory traces alive and then by keeping the facts of other people's lives available, first as individual biography and then as history. All these forms of writing center upon people's actions, motives, and interrelationships, in all their complexity and variety. History and biography are therefore among the most basic and enduring forms of writing and will certainly continue to be so. In tandem with this basic kind of writing is another form at least as old and honorable, and it is the use of writing to preserve for each new generation useful information and the accumulated knowledge about how to do things. This huge field now includes all textbooks, instruction manuals, compendiums of useful facts, dictionaries, guides, atlases, almanacs, and everything that we now think of as how-to-do-it books.

Textbooks comprise at least half of all the books published in America, yet this book is not going to tell you anything about how to write them. Almost all textbooks nowadays are the joint product of an established pedagogue and his editors at a textbook publishing house. As a result, the writing of textbooks at every level, from the simplest Dick and Jane reader all the way up to graduate texts in theoretical physics, is hemmed in and restricted to a degree that always makes the outsider blanch. The field is not open to the learner or to the writer trying to be published for the first time, and so we will leave it to the specialists whose careers and livelihood are tied up in it.

When it comes to how-to-do-it books that sell in the regular trade, however, the situation is almost reversed. Here anyone who has useful information that people may want to have and are willing to pay for can find a publisher, and many authors of these books don't even consider themselves writers. The key is the usefulness of the information and the clarity of its presentation.

Let us take a quite typical example. Mr. Edwin P. Alexander was, like thousands of other Americans, a railroad buff who devoted his life to their history, technology, and preservation. Having assembled model trains when still young, as an adult he became a very skillful model maker, supporting himself mostly by producing very superior and exact replicas of engines and cars.

Alexander was also, of course, a collector, and over the years he built up a vast store of everything to do with trains—pictures, drawings, plans, histories, memorabilia, ephemera such as tickets and schedules, and anything else connected with his subject. Using his archival material, he produced books on various train-related topics by selecting and organizing facts and photos he alone possessed. I published several of his books, of which *Down at the Depot: American Railroad Stations from 1831 to 1920* was quite typical. With over four hundred illustrations and a text consisting mainly of just the facts about each station pictured, it was a very successful book that pleased everyone, as did all his books. Nevertheless, he considered himself not a writer but an assembler of facts and pictures, and rightly so. The point is that no one else could produce the same facts, so by producing them he became a well-known author.

The rule is this: If you make yourself a leading expert in a field and then are able to present what you know in such a way that others will want it, you can and will be published. There should be no need for me to enumerate the kinds of how-to-do-it books and compendiums of information that are around: they're on display at the nearest bookstore for all to see. There you will find self-help books of every kind—diet books, books about a healthy mind—books that offer you knowledge about everything from improving your golf stroke to how to speak in public to how to land a job or analyze your insecurities. You can find books on subjects you hardly knew anyone cared about: how to gold leaf statues, how to build a hang glider, or how to project conic sections.

Although it always seems that there is already a book on any and every possible subject, every year hundreds of new books come out and many of them prove useful and popular. Part of the reason for this boom is that every year new fields open up or old ones expand. When I entered the book business there were hardly any books available on computers, for example, and now there are thousands of them. A dozen years ago windsurfing hardly existed and now it is an Olympic sport complete with all the trappings, including a number of books on it. Ten years ago only specialists in certain fields knew anything about various emerging scientific fields such as molecular biology, and as knowledge was gained so it was possible to put together a book.

But the emergence of a new subject for how-to-do-it books is by no means confined to new knowledge, for I can think of any number of books that I myself published that were on long-known subjects that had not been systematically treated before. I published a book on ephemeral folk figures—scarecrows, harvest figures, and snowmen—that was a great success. Adele Ernest did the first general trade book on American duck decoys, which had not been thought to be worth a whole book before that time, and it started a whole series of them. We did a book on carousel figures, circus wagons, and cigar store Indians—once again a field that no one had ever thought worthy of serious scholarship and attention. Twenty years ago would a subject such as, say, baseball cards have been worth a book? Today, as the cards themselves have become valuable collectors items there are books.

The passage of time confers historical importance on what used to seem like yesterday's junk. My mother's generation threw out all those Tiffany lamps that were cluttering up the living room, and it fell to a later time to realize their worth. When I published a book on Art Deco it seemed to many to be too near in time to be of any interest, yet the book was a great success, and many more books by other authors followed it. There is, of course, a natural cycle at work. Children tend to disparage and feel embarrassed by the things their parents bought and held in high esteem, feeling that what the old folks thought were the latest rage has now become nothing but yesterday's fad, and they put such things away and get their own things. It is only when the grandchildren are grown up that they look at their grandparents' things, now largely thrown out, and say, wait a minute. This cycle, it seems, takes about sixty years, and so in the 1990s the interests of the late 1930s and early 1940s should suddenly hold new fascination for the then new generation.

Some things, of course, don't change much. One of the earliest and most enduring of all how-to-do-it books was *A Sea Grammar* (1627), by Captain John Smith, which was not really superseded for 250 years. This strictly utilitarian manual of seamanship was enlivened by Smith's vigorous prose and made famous by his description of how to manage a fight at sea. From Smith's time until the later nineteenth century ships did not change all that much and neither did the names for the various parts of a ship and its rigging. Even the modern reader can recognize almost everything he mentions and his observations are as true now as when they were written:

The *rigging* [of] a Ship is all the *Ropes* or *Cordage* belonging to the Masts and Yards; and it is proper to say *The Mast is well rigged,* or, *The Yard is well rigged;* that is, when all the Ropes are well sised [sized] to a true proportion of her burthen. We say also, when they are too many or too great, *Shee is over-rigged,* and doth much wrong a Ship in her Sailing; for a small waight aloft is much more in that nature than a much greater below, and the more upright any Ship goeth, the better she saileth.

But where does this put the writer who wants to learn to write for publication? In thinking about this I have concluded that there isn't much point in trying to use comparisons of the *good, better, best* sort because the basic truth is that this kind of writing for the most part either works or it doesn't. That is, it is either clear or it isn't. Thus what an aspiring writer should study is a few good models of the sort of writing he is thinking of doing. Let us start by looking at one of the biggest categories of how-to-do-it books, a vast field that has made fortunes for both authors and publishers, and will always do so, for it touches upon a basic and necessary human function—eating, and cooking to eat.

My own interest in cookbooks started early, for when I was first married and moved into an apartment with my wife, I discovered that she had never been in a kitchen and didn't even know how to turn on a stove, much less boil water. I was amazed, but since I could do outdoor cooking and most of the things a short-order cook could do indoors, I found myself the chef of the house at the outset. When my wife got tired of my bacon and eggs, however, we got a couple of cookbooks and tried to expand our repertoire by reading them and trying different recipes. We quickly discovered that many recipes were so ambiguous that we could not use them. Some authors, so accustomed to the basics of doing things in a kitchen, assumed quite a lot of knowledge on the part of their readers, so we would read such phrases as "cook until done," "boil until tender," or "bake until brown," or "season to taste," and really not know what to do. It soon became evident that one cookbook that didn't assume anything but started you out at the beginning and took you as far as you cared to go, always with precise, accurate, and understandable directions, was *The Joy of Cooking*, by Irma S. Rombauer and Marion Rombauer Becker.

This famous publishing phenomenon was first printed by Bobbs-Merrill Company in 1931 and has been almost continuously revised and refined as it established itself as the best and best-selling cookbook of its day. Sales of it, which are still strong, sustained its publisher for many years until that company too fell to the modern wave of consolidation and agglomeration that has swept the industry. For almost sixty years now, it has been the preeminent cookbook, to be placed alongside the family Bible in the houses of those whose entire library consists of two books. My own mother had lived in households with servants until the time of World War II, when her cook left for a job in a factory; then, more than forty years of age, she too had to learn to cook by reading books. An intellectual woman who always basically hated cooking, she nonetheless wrote on the end-paper of the copy of *The Joy of Cooking* that I inherited from her: "I agree with dust jacket that this, despite its corny title, is *the* best all purpose cookbook. Dec. 1974."

But generalizations are of no use in this field, so let's plunge in and have a look at particulars. To this end I have chosen one of the simplest, most mundane, but most often repeated tasks that one is likely to find performed in the kitchen—and one with which I started my own married life—and that is making scrambled eggs. To start with, here is the recipe from *The Joy of Cooking:*

SCRAMBLED EGGS   2 Servings

Beaten egg whites may be added to whole eggs in the proportion of one additional white to 3 whole eggs.

Melt in a skillet over slow heat or in a well-greased double boiler ♦ over—not in—hot water:

1 tablespoon butter

Beat and pour in:

3 eggs
⅛ teaspoon salt
⅛ teaspoon paprika
(3 tablespoons cream)

When the eggs begin to thicken, break them into shreds with a fork or stir with a wooden spoon. When they have thickened, serve them on:

Hot toast lightly buttered or spread with fish paste, deviled ham or liver sausage; or in a hollowed-out hard roll

An attractive way to serve scrambled eggs is to put them in individual well-buttered ring molds while the eggs are still rather creamy in consistency. Let them finish cooking in their own heat, which will set them. Turn out and fill the center with any of the additions listed below.

Additions to Scrambled Eggs

Small amounts of the following may be stirred into the egg mixture before scrambling. They should be at least 70°.

Grated or crumbled cheese
Chopped, peeled, seeded, sautéed
   tomatoes flavored with basil
Cultured sour cream and chives
Canned chopped sardines
Crab meat, seasoned with
   curry powder
Capers
Chopped canned anchovies
Chopped sautéed onions
Crisp bacon bits
Small pieces of broiled sausage
Sautéed mushrooms
Poached calf brains

Now there are quite a few points worth noticing about all this. It packs a great deal of information in a small space and does so by using typography to its fullest extent. Ingredients are listed in bold face, optional items are in parentheses, and things that require special notice are marked with a small bold-face arrow—all conventions that save space and clarify the messages but do not intrude so much as to annoy. The recipe itself is widely flexible and yet what needs to be done is clear. The additions are listed in ascending order of complexity, and subrecipes like poached calf brains can be located with the index. For those novice cooks insecure about how to handle eggs, the authors provide a section called *Know Your Ingredients*. Here is how that is introduced:

> Oddly enough, many of the very basic cooking materials—those that go into ninety-nine out of a hundred recipes—are so familiar, or rather so constantly used, that their characteristics are taken for granted even by experienced cooks. And this is to say that, by beginners, their peculiarities are often simply ignored. Yet success in cooking largely depends on one's becoming fully aware of how grass roots ingredients react. Here and now we put them all—from butter to weather—under the enlarging glass and point out just what it is that they contribute to the cooking process. With the knowledge gained in this chapter and the chapter on Heat, plus the information keyed by symbol and reference into our recipes at the point of use, we assure you a continuous and steady development from would-be to sure-fire cook.

And here is how eggs are introduced:

ABOUT EGGS

Nothing stimulates the practiced cook's imagination like an egg.

Eggs can transform cake doughs by providing a structural framework for leaven, thicken custards and make them smooth, tenderize timbales and produce fine-grained ice creams. They bind gravies and mayonnaise; clarify or enrich soups; glaze rolls; insulate pie doughs against sogginess; create glorious meringues and souffles; and make ideal luncheon and emergency fare.

Because fresh eggs do all these things better than old eggs and because there is no comparison in taste and texture between the two ♦ always buy the very best quality you can find. It doesn't matter if their yolks are light or dark or if their shells are white or brown—as long as the shells are not shiny. While there is no test, except tasting, for good flavor ♦ the relative freshness of eggs may be determined by placing them in a large bowl of cold water. The ones that float are not usable.

This section is followed by *About Cooking Eggs, About Beating Eggs,* and *About Storing Eggs,* altogether making six columns of tightly packed information, including several illustrations. If there is anything a cook needs to know about eggs that is not in here, I cannot imagine what it might be.

In my view and in the view of generations of cooks, both beginner and expert, *The Joy of Cooking* is the standard against which all recipe directions should be measured. Since differences tend to be subtle, and since there are so many thousands of cookbooks, I have selected an example from each of three categories of cookbooks—those in the French style, the famous or nearly so, and the widely available—and will discuss them in roughly descending order of comprehensiveness and complexity.

Let's look first at the *Larousse Gastronomique.* This monument to French culture was first published in 1938 with an introduction by none other than "the king of cooks and the cook of kings"—Auguste Escoffier. Compiled by Prosper Montagne and containing well over a million words, it was not until 1961 that several translators and editors produced the English-language edition I have, which was published by Hamlyn in London. It is, of course, arranged as an encyclopedia, alphabetically, and the entries are very comprehensive indeed. To find yet another scrambled-egg recipe, we start at "Eggs." There we find "Eggs, Basic Recipes" and, reading down the boldface entries, "Boiled eggs (hard boiled)," "Boiled eggs (soft boiled)," "Eggs en cocotte, cassolettes, ou caissettes," "Eggs à la coque," "Fried eggs," "Eggs in a mould," "Poached eggs," and then "Scrambled eggs." Here is that entry:

Scrambled eggs. OEUFS BROUILLÉS—Well prepared scrambled eggs are a very delicious dish, but it is vital that they should be cooked with care—they must be smooth and creamy.

Like an omelette, scrambled eggs can be garnished in various ways.

First method. The following quantities are enough for four people. Choose a small frying pan with a thick bottom or a small saucepan. Melt 3 tablespoons (50 grams) of butter. Break 8 eggs and beat *lightly* as for an omelette. Season and put in the pan.

Cook over a low heat, i.e. on the corner of the stove and stir constantly with a wooden spoon.

Gather into the middle the parts of the eggs which have been cooked on the sides of the pan. When the eggs are cooked, remove them from the stove and add 4 tablespoons (60 grams) of butter cut into small pieces. Mix well and keep hot in a *bain-marie* (pan of hot water) until the moment of serving.

Serving. Garnish according to the recipe chosen and serve in a pie dish or in a vegetable dish.

Second method. Use a double saucepan. Fill the larger pan half way up with warm water. Put the butter and the beaten eggs in the smaller pan. Cook over a low heat, stirring with a wooden spoon.

When the eggs are cooked, add butter, cut into small pieces as described above.

Note. According to the recipe chosen, two or three tablespoons of fresh cream can be added to scrambled eggs after they are cooked.

Scrambled eggs can be served in small or large *croustades** made from puff pastry, in *timbales** made from best plain pastry, in *cassolettes**, in hollowed out vegetables or in metal or china pie dishes.

But this is by no means all: it is followed shortly by the entry "Scrambled Eggs a l'américaine"—

> **Scrambled eggs a l'américaine.** OEUFS BROUILLÉS A L'AMÉRICAINE—Add diced bacon, fried in butter, to the scrambled eggs. Heap the eggs on a warm platter and garnish with rashers of grilled bacon and halved grilled tomatoes.
>
> *Note.* The same name also applies to scrambled eggs with sliced lobster (or spiny lobster a l'americaine). Recipes for these dishes will be found under entry entitled *Scrambled eggs a l'américaine.*

—and then this is followed by no less then thirty-four *other* ways to make scrambled eggs. There is good reason for *Larousse* to claim to be an encyclopedia. I took the trouble to count the total number of egg recipes, and there are 243, not counting omelette recipes, of which there are 114.

Larousse may have overused typographical conventions to clarify and sort things out—boldface, full capital letters, italic, and asterisks—but even so the entries are clear enough if one is not a beginner. But the usual French assumption of prior knowledge is everywhere evident:

> **Scrambled eggs with shrimps.** OEUFS BROUILLÉS AUX CREVETTES—Add to the eggs some peeled shrimps' tails heated in butter. Heap on a warm platter. Garnish the top with a little mound of shrimps' tails heated in butter or in Shrimp Sauce (see SAUCE). Surround with croutons cut in the shape of wolves' teeth fried in butter. Pour a ring of Shrimp sauce round the eggs.

This supposes that one naturally picks the necessary number of shrimp and that the croutons cut in the shape of wolves' teeth have been fried in butter at just the right moment so that they are warm and crispy when the eggs are ready. The book implies that at least a couple of *sous-chefs* are at one's beck and call.

All this should be enough to give the reader the general flavor of *Larousse*. Its old-fashioned air—"cook over a low heat, i.e. on the corner of the stove"—indicates that the writer does not envision the reader having a stove with individual burners. Nevertheless, most cooks I have spoken to use it when they are thinking of *grand cuisine* and feel able to cope with such complexities.

But since the aim of this chapter is instruction and not judgment, let us forge ahead. After *Larousse,* the book with the most similar pretensions is perhaps *The Gourmet Cookbook,* assembled by the staff of *Gourmet* magazine and first published in 1950. This cookbook is simpler than *Larousse*—there are a mere four entries under scrambled eggs—and the basic instructions are straightforward.

> ***Scrambled Eggs.*** Scrambled eggs should be cooked over very slow heat in a heavy copper or cast-iron skillet. The basic procedure is as follows: For 4 servings, break at least 8 eggs into a bowl and beat them with a fork sufficiently to blend the whites and yolks thoroughly without whipping up a froth. Season to taste with salt and white pepper. Melt over a very low flame 2 tablespoons butter or bacon fat and before it begins to bubble, pour in the egg mass. As the eggs coagulate on the bottom and at the edges of the pan, pull the solids to the center to let the parts that are still liquid take their place. Keep moving and blending liquid and solid until all has become firm but is still moist. Remove the pan from the fire and while the heat retained by the pan does the final cooking, scramble the eggs rapidly and serve them immediately. The eggs will be firm, soft, custardy, not dry and leathery.
>
> Before beating the eggs, a little milk or water may be added to delay further the cooking of the eggs.

Interestingly enough, one of the other full entries is for scrambled eggs with shrimp:

Oeufs Brouillés Mariette. Scrambled Eggs with Shrimp. Have ready 6 eggs, slightly beaten with 3 tablespoons cream, 1 cup shrimp, cooked and shelled, 2 medium-sized tomatoes, peeled, seeded, and chopped, 2 shallots, finely chopped, 2 mushroom caps, finely sliced, and butter.

Melt 6 tablespoons butter in the top pan of the chafing dish over hot water. Add the shallots and mushrooms and simmer for 4 to 5 minutes, stirring occasionally. Then add the shrimp and tomatoes and heat for 1 minute, stirring gently. Pour in the beaten eggs and stir slowly until they are thick and creamy. Salt to taste, pour the mixture over squares of buttered toast, and dust with grated cheese.

Here we do not have croutons cut in the shape of wolves' teeth but squares of buttered toast. We do have two medium-sized tomatoes, peeled, seeded, and chopped, which may be equal in trouble to shaping croutons, but the directions are easily understood and without explicit variations. Note that the shrimp recipe is in a section that is about chafing-dish cooking and thus the recipe is expected to be done in a chafing dish. There are no typographical aids beyond the placement of the recipe title in the margin of the entry. Quantities are specified as well as cooking times. All in all, it is remarkably direct for a book that is supposed to be for gourmets.

Now we turn to "regular" cookbooks; that is, ones written by individuals rather than by a committee or a large corporate sponsor. *Mastering the Art of French Cooking,* by Julia Child, Louisette Bertholle, and Simone Beck, is perhaps the best-known book of its type to have been published in the last generation, probably owing to Julia Child's regular television appearances. It is a fine example of its genre and has been very widely used. At the start in "A Note on the Recipes" the authors explain their general methods:

All of the master recipes and most of the subrecipes in this book are in two-column form. On the left are the ingredients, often including some special piece of equipment needed; on the right is a paragraph of instruction. Thus what to cook and how to cook it, at each step in the proceedings, are always brought together in one sweep of the eye. Master recipes are headed in large, bold type; a special sign, *, precedes those which are followed by variations. Most of the recipes contain this sign, (*), in the body of the text, indicating up to what point a dish may be prepared in advance. Wine and vegetable suggestions are included with all master recipes for main-course dishes.

Our primary purpose in this book is to teach you how to cook, so that you will understand the fundamental techniques and gradually be able to divorce yourself from a dependence on recipes.

Then on to the recipe:

*SCRAMBLED EGGS
[Oeufs Brouillés]

Scrambled eggs in French are creamy soft curds that just hold their shape from fork to mouth. Their preparation is entirely a matter of stirring the eggs over gentle heat until they slowly thicken as a mass into a custard. No liquid or liquid-producing ingredients such as tomatoes should be beaten into them before cooking, as this is liable to turn them watery.

For 4 or 5 servings

A fork or a wire whip
8 eggs, or 7 eggs and 2 yolks
A mixing bowl
¼ tsp salt
Pinch of pepper

Beat the eggs in the bowl with the seasonings for 20 to 30 seconds to blend yolks and whites.

2 Tb softened butter **A heavy-bottomed,** **enameled, pyrex,** **earthenware or** **stainless steel** **saucepan or** **skillet 7 to 8** **inches in** **diameter. Depth of** **eggs in pan** **should be 2/3 to 1** **inch.** **A rubber spatula,** **wooden spoon, or** **wire whip**	Smear the bottom and sides of the pan with the butter. Pour in the eggs and set over moderately low heat. Stir slowly and continually, reaching all over the bottom of the pan. Nothing will seem to happen for 2 to 3 minutes as the eggs gradually heat. Suddenly they will begin to thicken into a custard. Stir rapidly, moving pan on and off heat, until the eggs have almost thickened to the consistency you wish. Then remove from heat, as they will continue to thicken slightly.

1½ to 2 Tb softened **butter or** **whipping cream** **A warm buttered** **platter** **Parsley sprigs**	Just as soon as they are of the right consistency, stir in the enrichment butter or cream, which will stop the cooking. Season to taste, turn out onto the platter, decorate with parsley, and serve. (*) The eggs may be kept for a while in their saucepan over tepid water, but the sooner they are served the better.

This cookbook is pretty sophisticated, but it is not as flexible as Rombauer and Becker's, and its use of special typographical conventions is somewhat less extensive than theirs, but Child is one of the few authors who will tell you what utensils and equipment are needed as well as giving the actual ingredients. The recipe itself is followed by several variations—*Aux Fines Herbes, Au Fromage, Aux Truffes,* and *Garnishings.* The system of giving a basic recipe and then encouraging variations seems well designed to do what the authors intended: to set the cook free from specific recipes.

One of Child's co-authors, Louisette Bertholle, later published her own book, *French Cuisine for All,* and it is interesting to see how its format varies from that of the earlier

volume. There is no special introductory material, so we
will just look at what she has to say about scrambled eggs.

SCRAMBLED EGGS *Les oeufs brouillés*

Scrambled eggs, unlike omelets, must be cooked
slowly over low heat. At the end of cooking they
should look creamy and slightly lumpy. The most
foolproof way to cook them is over a pan of simmering water or in a double boiler. If you are really
expert, you may cook them without setting them
over hot water, but by using a heavy-bottomed enam-
eled saucepan set on an asbestos mat. Eggs have an
odd way of shrinking when scrambled, so you must
allow three or four eggs per person. For six people
make two separate batches. Have your utensils near
at hand: a fork, a wooden spatula, and a wire whisk.

Scrambled Eggs, Basic Recipe   *for 3 people*

3 tablespoons butter plus 2–3 pats of cold butter
10 very fresh eggs
a few drops of water (no more than a teaspoon)
salt
freshly ground white pepper

Melt the butter in the saucepan or in the top of a double
boiler. Crack the eggs into a large bowl, add the water, salt,
and pepper. Beat the eggs rapidly with a fork until the
yolks and whites are just blended. Pour the eggs into the
saucepan, place on top of the simmering water over moderate heat. With a wooden spatula stir the eggs with a
smooth, wide, regular, circular motion, the spatula touching the bottom of the pan. For one or two minutes nothing
will seem to happen, the mixture will not seem to be thick-
ening. With patience, continue to work with the spatula
without increasing speed, and suddenly the eggs will start
to thicken and a few lumps will appear. Stir a little faster,
scraping down the bits of egg on the sides of the pan.
Remove it from the heat, and with the whisk beat in the
pats of cold butter one after the other. This will stop the
cooking and make the eggs shine. Place the eggs immediately onto a warmed metal dish, then serve on warmed
plates.

For a more elaborate presentation, scrambled eggs may

be served on Canapes* or in Croustades.* If you serve them on canapes, accompany them with a few slices of crisply fried bacon or a bowl of Tomato Sauce.*

This is followed by three recipes for variations:

SCRAMBLED EGGS ON CANAPES WITH ASPARAGUS TIPS *Canapes d'oeufs brouillés aux pointes d'asperges*

A delicate hot hors-d'oeurve.   *For 6 canapes*

> **6 canapes made of 6 slices homemade white bread and 4–5 tablespoons margarine**
> **1½ pounds slender green asparagus**
> **2–3 tablespoons butter**
> **salt**
> **freshly ground pepper**
> **Scrambled Eggs, Basic Recipe***

Prepare the canapes in advance. Cut the crusts from the bread and discard them, sauté the slices in the margarine until they are very lightly browned. Set on paper towels to drain, sprinkle lightly with salt.

Wash, peel, and cut off the tips of the asparagus to a length of 1½ inches (the stalks can be used in soup). Stew the tips in the butter turning them carefully with a fork, until they are tender. Salt and pepper them, keep them warm.

Cook the eggs, distribute them on the reheated canapes, and garnish with the asparagus tips.

CROUSTADES WITH SCRAMBLED EGGS AND TRUFFLES *Croustades d'oeufs brouillés aux truffes*

One canned small truffle gives this elegant first course its magic touch. Make the croustades the day before, cover them, and store in the refrigerator.   *For 6 people*

> **Scrambled Eggs, Basic Recipe* (10–12 eggs)**
> **1 small truffle, sliced fine**
> **truffle juice**
> **6 Croustades***

Prepare the scrambled eggs. Add the truffle juice along with the reserved pats of butter (in basic recipe) at the end of cooking. Fill the reheated croustades with the eggs and garnish each one with a thin slice of truffle.

MOLDED RICE PILAF WITH SCRAMBLED EGGS AND TOMATO SAUCE *Couronne de riz aux oeufs brouillés accompagnee de sauce tomate*

You will need a ring mold for preparing this delicious, colorful dish.

For 6 people (if served as a first course)
For 4 people (if served as a light meal)

5 cups cooked Rice Pilaf* (a little underdone, as it will cook more in the mold)
Scrambled Eggs, Basic Recipe*
2 cups well-seasoned Tomato Sauce*

Put the pilaf in a buttered ring mold, place the mold over a pan of boiling water on medium heat for 10 minutes. While the rice is cooking, prepare the scrambled eggs. Heat the tomato sauce. Unmold the rice on a warmed round plate and fill the center with the hot scrambled eggs. Serve the tomato sauce in a bowl.

In general the whole cookbook is less elaborate and less open to variation but entirely clear and, as one would expect, in a spirit very close to Child's.

Let us look for our last example at a typical series book— in this case *The Gourmet's Guide to French Cooking,* by Alison Burt. This is a rather short book full of color plates (fifty) and lots (sixty-two) of black and white photographs, so there isn't all that much room for recipes. It's a kind of coffee-table book, put out to look good and sell for an attractive price, and makes no pretense of being comprehensive. Here is the only scrambled-egg recipe in the book:

Oeufs brouillés aux tomatoes
Scrambled eggs with tomatoes

2 tomatoes
1 tablespoon (1¼ T) olive oil

1 shallot, finely chopped
1 oz. (2T) butter
1 tablespoon (1¼ T) milk
4 eggs
salt and pepper
chopped parsley for garnish

Blanche the tomatoes in boiling water, remove skin and pips. Chop roughly. Heat the olive oil in a small saucepan, fry the shallot until it has softened then add the tomatoes. Cook for 2–3 minutes, stirring constantly.

Melt the butter in a saucepan. Beat the milk and eggs together and season. Add the eggs to the butter and cook, stirring constantly over a low heat, until the mixture is creamy.

Place the scrambled eggs on a heated dish, make a hollow in the centre. Spoon the tomato mixture on to the eggs and garnish with finely chopped parsley.

Serve immediately.

Serves 4.

Now that we probably never want to think about scrambled eggs again, what have we learned? All of these recipes have their uses, that a cook using any one of them would be better off than one working without any directions at all, so which is best is pretty much a matter of taste. Some of these books offer an approach more open to experiment and variation, but any one of them is understandable and capable of actually being carried out. That is the fundamental point. Do these classic, typical how-to-do-it examples really tell how to do it? The answer is yes, they do. There is no pure and perfect way to accomplish this end, so each set of instructions must be measured against a simple standard— does it work? If it does, then it will serve.

If that is as close as we may care to look at how specific sets of instruction work, the next thing to ask is, How do writers handle matters that are not so precise?

All of the foregoing examples and comment have been

about matters of instruction, and all how-to-do-it books are books specifically of instruction. The best way to learn how to write clear instructions is to study good models in whatever field you yourself wish to work. I advise the reader of this book who wishes to write in this form to study examples that are as close as possible to what you yourself want to do. Of course that is shameless copying, in a sense, but I do not mean to imply that you should copy facts as well as style. Develop your own facts and use them in a style that you know is clear, straightforward, and comprehensive.

There are, of course, whole reams of books about things that are muddy and hard to make precise, and some have been very great best-sellers. Dale Carnegie's *How to Win Friends and Influence People* was probably the most famous of this sort of thing, but Norman Vincent Peale's *Power of Positive Thinking* probably runs it a close second. I do not myself have much use for this sort of pop-psychology self-help book and think that only people with a certain cast of mind can write such things successfully. I do know that the writer himself has to be a believer or it won't work. No cynical attempt by someone who thinks it is all drivel will in fact be convincing, and the reader is urged not to try. If someone has really found a way to train people so that they can take up public speaking and become successful at it, then perhaps he can write a how-to-speak-in-public book— but he had better really have something new to say, for in this field, as in others, mere exhortations have been tried plenty of times before and they are never enough.

HOW THINGS WORK

ONE STEP ABOVE SIMPLE INSTRUCTION is explanation. To explain something, at the very minimum a writer has to know his subject well enough to make sense out of it for someone else. Before we launch into the details of the matter, let me digress.

When I was in college in the late 1940s I always had in mind the question What is going to be the most exciting field in the world in the next fifty years? I was a writer and editor already and also a history and philosophy student, but I still thought that I would like to spend my working life on whatever was going to be the most interesting and dynamic development that would take place during my lifetime. History would always interest me, but I could come back to it, and philosophy didn't look as if it were going anywhere: it had been reduced largely to verbal quibbling and the hot new field of existentialism was little more than an open acknowledgment that no one had an answer to David Hume. Most businesses were dull or worse, and certainly would not form the character of the age. No, plainly the central endeavor of the age would be science.

The stunning success of the atomic bomb had virtually guaranteed that science would be well financed in the coming years, and though there was no telling where it would all lead, it certainly seemed that we were on the threshold of a huge explosion in all of the sciences, and most especially in physics. My two roommates were both physics students, and some of my other friends were premed students or anthropology, and geology majors. I looked at all these fields and concluded, after trying several courses, that I did not have the aptitude for science. I could not do mathematics, I was bored by compendia of facts such as those taught in geology, and I refused to learn to speak and write German, which was then regarded as essential for serious study in physics. I also realized that I did not have the first-class mind I considered a prerequisite for a physicist. In this I was, of course, wrong, since most of the people I knew who later were quite successful in physics didn't have first-class minds either. So, somewhat to my dismay, I concluded that science was what would be going on in my time, and yet I would not be part of it.

Here, it should be noted, I accepted my limitations. In the end it was well that I did, for as we shall shortly see, I later did what I considered the next best thing—I helped to bring science to a larger public. But at the time it meant that my interest in science would remain that of an outsider. But I found satisfaction in accepting and working within my limits; trying to do what I had no talent for had brought me nothing but frustration.

In the early 1950s, as a book editor at Doubleday I was still deeply interested in science but I had no outlet for that interest. Great things were indeed going on in science, but it seemed that the general public was not being told about it. At the time such professional journals as the weekly *Science,* which was as close to a general-interest science magazine as was being published, were written in strictly professional prose. Laymen found the jargon impregnable, and even scientists found articles outside their field hard to understand. Science news was being published all right, in this as in thousands of other journals, but it was all technical and written for people who were already specialists themselves. Authors did not trouble to indicate the implications or the relative importance of any new finding, and in fact seemed happy enough to keep the public out.

The one great exception to this state of affairs was *Scientific American,* a magazine that, although written by scientists, attempted to tell what was going on in the various areas of science in layman's English. The magazine's ideal reader was another scientist, but one from another discipline. A mathematician was a layman when it came to molecular biology, and a high-energy physicist was a layman when it came to population dynamics, but they were all working scientists: they all understood proper ideas about rigor and necessary levels of proof and control experiments and the reproducibility of experimental evidence and the basic notions of what constituted science in the first place. I thought that the magazine did a wonderful and a very important job, but when I tried to enlist several of its scientist-authors to do books I ran into a huge obstacle.

Apparently scientists thought of themselves as a sort of priesthood, the possessors of esoteric knowledge that would only be distorted if one attempted to explain it to an outsider. They considered journalists to be sensation-mongers and distorters of truth, although they accepted *Scientific American* because it was written by scientists *for* scientists—that was all right. But whenever they tried to explain a scientific concept, for example, to a newspaper reporter, they felt that what their ideas were was always grossly twisted and conclusions were always drawn that were not justified by the facts. I was repeatedly rebuffed in my efforts to get scientists to either write about what they were doing themselves—so as to avoid such distortions—or else talk to responsible journalists about what was going on. My persistence was finally rewarded when, after reading a good piece in *Scientific American,* I convinced its author, John R. Pierce, to do a book.

Pierce was not an academic, a point of great importance. He was director of research for electrical communications at the Bell Telephone Laboratories in Murray Hill, New

Jersey. At that lab Claude Shannon had written his classic *The Mathematical Theory of Communication* (1949), and there the transistor had been invented, a feat that earned its progenitors the Nobel Prize. Bell Labs was not afraid of the public and quite aware that it was supported by a profit-making telephone company. But the labs were a wonderful place to do science, because if the people who ran the place, who were scientists themselves, thought that an investigation was worthwhile, it was okayed. Pierce would do a book on electronics because he wanted to get it right and understood that if he didn't tell it in all its correctness, then others were likely to get it wrong. The result was *Electronics: Waves and Messages,* published in 1956.

The Pierce book was for me a great breakthrough, for it helped me to convince other scientists that if they didn't write about what they were doing, then others would, and would likely do the subject a disservice. It also gave me the freedom to do what I wanted inside Doubleday, for the Pierce book was, to the great surprise of the publishing house, a fine commercial success. That book got me started as a science editor and later led to, among other things, the founding of The Natural History Press.

And why should this long story be of interest to someone who is trying to learn to write for publication? Because it leads to a consideration of writing books about science for nonscientists, a difficult form of explanation. Writing about science for laymen is still a new field, having only grown up in the last thirty years, but it is full of importance, excitement, and the meaning of the most important endeavor of our age.

It is perhaps hard to realize just how far science writing has come in the last forty years. Right after the war some of the great classics of modern science were being published, but they were strictly hard science and made no concessions at all to those who were not technically capable of reading them. *Theory of Games and Economic Behavior,* by John von Neumann and Oskar Morgenstern, for example, was an enormously influential book, but it took years for the ideas in it to radiate outward from the small circle of specialists who were able to read it. Now, to the astonishment of old hands like me, I see as I write this that a serious book about science is at the top of the best-seller list: *A Brief History of Time: From the Big Bang to Black Holes,* by Stephen W. Hawking.

The success of *A Brief History of Time* would have been impossible even fifteen years ago, but now people everywhere seem willing to think about the deep questions of our time—and serious scientists are willing and able to write about them. Whether all this is due to the vast publicity given to the space program, the heroism of Hawking's struggle against his illness, or a much higher level of sophistication about science on the part of a much better educated public I couldn't say, but the situation certainly is to be applauded. That is, in fact, what I started working for in the 1950s. It is gratifying to realize that many others have come to feel as I did then and that the state of science writing is very much changed as a result.

Today there are several kinds of science writing. First is professional writing, the kind that is in *Science* and in the specialist journals in every field, which uses technical jargon and is not intended for outsiders. The second can be characterized by the type of articles in *Scientific American,* which do not slur over difficulties and complications but use straight English and is expected to be understandable to the hypothetical "educated layman." The many books like *A Brief History of Time* that are now being published on scientific subjects are examples of this level of writing. Third is the science journalism that we can read in, for example, the *Science* section of the *New York Times.* As journalists have become better educated in science, their writing about science has become more accurate, more responsible, and more important. A science-based story on the front page of a daily newspaper is no longer a surprise. But science journalism has relatively few practitioners and is confined mostly to magazines and newspapers, and we are, as usual, concerning ourselves mostly with books.

At this point we shall have to do for science what we did for cooking, which means finding a subject that a number of writers have tried to explain to see how their methods differ. To that end I have picked what might be called the scrambled eggs of science writing: the Doppler shift.

To plunge right in, we shall start with an article from *World Monitor* (November 1988) by Alan Lightman, a physicist at the Smithsonian Astrophysical Observatory and professor of science and writing at MIT, which includes his explanation of the Doppler shift:

> Velocities of moving stars, and indeed of most astronomical objects, are measured by the shift in their colors, the so called (sic) Doppler shift. Just as the whistle of a train rises in pitch as the train moves toward us and falls as the train moves away, so the color of an approaching star shifts upward in frequency, toward the blue end of the spectrum, and the color of a receding star shifts down, toward the red. The speed of the star can be found from the amount of the shift.

In addition to this clear, concise explanation, the article includes a four-color illustration showing how the shift works, with stars at one end being red and then shifting through orange to yellow to yellow-green to green to blue-green to solid blue. Whether this is really needed is hard to say, but anyone reading the explanation and seeing the illustration really ought to get the idea.

Let us take another example, this time from James Trefil's *The Dark Side of the Universe:*

> Important as Hubble's proof of the existence of other galaxies was, another discovery he made as part of the same study was even more striking. Looking out at nearby galaxies, Hubble could see that they were moving away from him, and that the farther away the galaxy was, the faster it was moving. This discovery is so astounding—so fraught with implications for

modern cosmology—that we should consider the basis of the reasoning on which Hubble made his claim.

When you stand next to a highway and hear a car blowing its horn as it goes by, you notice that the sound of the horn changes when the car passes you. Its pitch is higher as the car approaches, lower as it moves away. This is an example of what is called the Doppler effect. It is explained most easily by reference to Fig. 1.

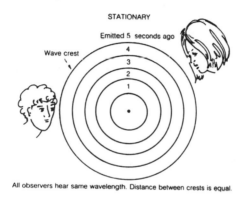

STATIONARY

Emitted 5 seconds ago

Wave crest

All observers hear same wavelength. Distance between crests is equal.

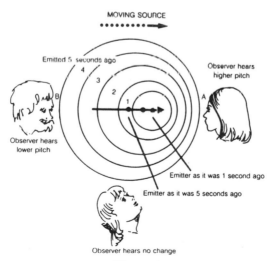

MOVING SOURCE

Emitted 5 seconds ago

Observer hears higher pitch

Observer hears lower pitch

Emitter as it was 1 second ago

Emitter as it was 5 seconds ago

Observer hears no change

Figure 1

When a stationary car emits a sound wave, as in the top diagram of Fig. 1, a series of concentric rings of compressions and rarefactions in the air move out from the car. When these strike our ear we hear a sound, and its pitch depends on how closely bunched the waves are. The more waves that strike our ear each second, the higher the pitch.

If the car is moving, as in the bottom diagram, then it will actually travel some small distance between the time it emits one wave and the time it emits another. Each wave will be centered on the spot where the car was when that particular wave was emitted. The result is that the formerly concentric pattern is replaced by the skewed pattern shown. Someone standing at point A when the car is approaching will perceive the waves to be more closely packed than normal. That observer will hear a sound of higher pitch. At B, however, the waves are less closely packed than normal and the observer hears a sound of lower pitch.

This explains the Doppler effect, and it also explains how Hubble discovered the expansion of the universe.

Although Trefil, a professor of physics at George Mason University in Fairfax, Virginia, is the author of several other books and is regarded as an outstanding writer about science, his explanation is somewhat labored and the illustration he uses hardly helps matters.

In *A Brief History of Time,* Stephen Hawking gives a very good and perhaps a more satisfactory explanation:

In the 1920's, when astronomers began to look at the spectra of stars in other galaxies, they found something most peculiar: there were the same characteristic sets of missing colors as for stars in our own galaxy, but they were all shifted by the same relative amount toward the red end of the spectrum. To understand the implications of this, we must first understand the Doppler effect. As we have seen, visible light consists of fluctuations, or waves, in the electromagnetic field. The frequency (or number of waves per second) of light is extremely high, ranging from four to seven hundred million million waves per second. The different frequencies of light are what the human eye sees as different colors, with the lowest frequencies appearing at the red end of the spectrum and the highest frequencies at the blue end. Now imagine a source of light at a constant distance from us, such as a star, emitting waves of light at a constant frequency. Obviously the frequency of the waves we receive will be the same as the frequency at which they are emitted (the gravitational field of the galaxy will not be large enough to have a significant effect). Suppose now that the source starts moving toward us. When the source emits the next wave crest it will be nearer to us, so the time that wave crest takes to reach us will be less than when the star was stationary. This means that the time between the two wave crests reaching us is smaller, and therefore the number of waves we receive each second (i.e., the frequency) is higher than when the star was stationary.

Correspondingly, if the source is moving away from us, the frequency of the waves we receive will be lower. In the case of light, therefore, this means that stars moving away from us will have their spectra shifted toward the red end of the spectrum (red-shifted) and those moving toward us will have their spectra blue-shifted. This relationship between frequency and speed, which is called the Doppler effect, is an everyday experience. Listen to a car passing on the road: as the car is approaching, its engine sounds at a higher pitch (corresponding to a higher frequency of sound waves), and when it passes and goes away, it sounds at a lower pitch. The behavior of light or radio waves is similar. Indeed, the police make use of the Doppler effect to measure the speed of cars by measuring the frequency of pulses of radio waves reflected off them.

This explanation seems preferable to the previous one, but here too each reader must judge for himself. Hawking holds Isaac Newton's chair as Lucasian Professor of Mathematics at Cambridge University, England, and as the book jacket says, he "is widely regarded as the most brilliant theoretical physicist since Einstein." He has spent the last twenty years trapped in a wheelchair suffering from Lou Gehrig's disease and yet has managed to do groundbreaking research into black holes and other deep puzzles of modern physics. That he was willing to write a book for a popular audience and did so is a remarkable testament to the current attitude that serious scientists have toward not only their work but toward the public. The fact that the book became a best-seller is equally remarkable, and I think it makes this book a genuine landmark in publishing history. It is a measure of how science has penetrated every corner of our lives and of how we have come to accept that; how education has not only improved in the last generation but is more widespread; how increasingly sophisticated the so-called layman and book-buying public have become; and how the market for science writing has grown.

But let us take another example. Here is the relevant passage from *Perfect Symmetry: The Search for the Beginning of Time,* by Heinz R. Pagels:

Hubble's work on galaxies led him to make an important further contribution to an understanding of the expansion of the universe, something on which many people had speculated before him. Like many major discoveries, the discovery of the expansion of the universe did not come all at once. The way was prepared during the years 1912 to 1923 by Vesto Slipher, the American astronomer, who made careful measurements of the shift in the color of light emitted by nearby galaxies. He found that most galaxies had light that shifted toward the red. We know that light emitted by an object moving away from us shifts to lower frequencies corresponding to red, just as a train horn sounds lower as it moves away—an effect called the Doppler shift. So the simplest interpretation of Slipher's "red shift" is that most galaxies are moving away from us—a strange conclusion if one conceived of the galaxies as moving about randomly in the space of the universe.

Pagels, who died tragically in the summer of 1988 in a mountaineering accident, had been executive director of The New York Academy of Sciences and adjunct professor at The Rockefeller University. He was not only at the forefront of thinkers about the deepest questions about the universe, he was also a gifted writer who was willing both to explain his science and to speculate on ultimate meanings. Anyone who thinks about the big bang for any length of time is going to ask what was there before the big bang, why the laws of physics are as they are and not some other way, and several similar questions. These questions do not have answers in any normal sense, and so thinking about them might be termed theological, but plenty of physicists simply turn off when these kinds of questions loom nearby, while Pagels confronted them directly.

In any case, we have seen four distinguished professional scientists who are only secondarily writers explain the Doppler shift. Each of them has, in my view, given an understandable account of that basic point of astronomy. As a contrast to these descriptions, let's consider a more "academic" style of writing—the kind of writing that one would find in a textbook.

Here is an excerpt from Robert K. Adair's *The Great Design: Particles, Fields, and Creation:*

> If a tuning fork is set in vibration and emits sound, an identical tuning fork nearby will absorb some of the sound in resonance, begin vibrating, and reemit the sound. Atoms and nuclei act similarly. If the excited samarium nucleus emits electromagnetic waves of a particular frequency as a high-energy gamma-ray photon of definite energy, another (identical) samarium is moving away from the second (absorbing) tuning fork with an appreciable velocity, the frequency of the sound at the absorbing fork will be reduced by a Doppler effect, and no resonance absorption and reradiation will occur. Similarly, although the emitting fork is fixed, if the absorbing fork moves away, that

fork will "hear" a lower note, and again there will be no resonance absorption of the sound.

Now this is not an explanation of the Doppler shift, but a use of it to explain another point. Adair, the associate director for high energy and nuclear physics at the Brookhaven National Laboratory and Eugene Higgins Professor of Physics at Yale University, a distinguished man indeed, makes few concessions to the needs of the uninitiated. In fact, he expects his readers to already know what a Doppler shift is. Although it was purportedly designed for the layman, this book is actually more of a textbook in advanced physics; it does not shy from the proper mathematical formulations of the concepts discussed, and, in fact, equations appear on most pages. There is nothing wrong with this, of course—serious students *must* have the proper mathematical approach—but it does seem to be too much for most nonspecialists. I have included it here only to show that there are several levels of science writing; a pure textbook would make even fewer concessions than Adair does here. So when I talk about science writing I mean writing for a general, unscientific audience.

What have we learned from all this? I think that the most important point is that when it comes to complicated scientific matters, there are lots of ways of explaining any given concept, and, as with the scrambled-eggs examples, there is no one perfect way to do things. What is required is a writer who is thoroughly steeped in his subject and who has a clear head and a direct writing style.

But we cannot leave a consideration of science writing without noting what I think is its great importance. Few people would contest the statement that the whole modern ecology movement, including the establishment of the environmental protection agencies of the government, were given a tremendous impetus by the writings of Rachel Carson. *Silent Spring* (1962) had a sort of power that penetrated people's consciences over a period of time and gradually changed the whole way that they looked at the natural world. It is certainly simplistic to claim that *Uncle Tom's Cabin* precipitated the Civil War or that *Silent Spring* created the environmental movement, but each of those books was emblematic of a major shift in public awareness.

In the past generation so many wonderful scientific books have been written that I cannot even mention many of them, let alone use excerpts from them, but anyone wishing to read the best of what has been around should at once investigate the works of Loren Eiseley, Stephen Jay Gould, Gregory Bateson, and Lewis Thomas. They are all perfectly splendid writers and any one of them can stand as a model to be admired and emulated. They are all in what I think of as the romantic mold of science writing. That is, they seem to feel themselves *in* nature, not outside it looking coolly in, and to have an almost mystical feeling of oneness with the dim pulses of life and the slow, implacable processes of the mountains and the seas. Their thought is no less rigorously scientific for being essentially reverential in its approach to the world. It is curious but nonetheless true that these people are emotionally closer to primitive peoples in their attitudes than they are to priests and theologians. Perhaps, with them, we will all learn to become closer to nature and return to feelings that were given up with the coming of formal, structured religious ideas.

In any case it should be clear by now that I regard good science writing as the highest form of modern writing. The readers of this book will hardly be able to attempt it unless they already know a field in considerable depth, but that is no reason to fail to appreciate it as a very important and challenging form, to be emulated if possible but appreciated if not. As it turned out, science has indeed been the most exciting enterprise of the age, and it behooves us all to try to understand as much of it as we can, for it is what is shaping our lives now and will continue to shape the lives of our children for the foreseeable future.

Giving instructions and explanations is one of the most basic, most important functions of all writing. If a would-be author who knows his subject is willing to practice, it is not hard to learn.

Style

AND

SUBSTANCE

So FAR IN THIS BOOK we have paid no attention to style. We have assumed that what was needed was clarity and that the author proceeds without any consciousness of the manner in which he writes. We have, in fact, assumed not only that all writers use a "no style" style, but that this effect is easy to achieve. The truth is, of course, that such a style of writing is both difficult and seldom achieved. We need to take a brief look at it.

The basic idea of the "no style" style is that the writer's method should not be apparent, that the words serve as a transparent medium between the writer's thoughts and the reader's perception of them. If writing is a window through which we look to see the writer's mind, then what we want is not a dirty window or a smudged pane of glass, but a most expensive sort of invisible glass. Newspaper reporters are supposed to write in such a way, although few of them actually do. Here, though, is a sample of the style in its pure form:

From the *Providence Journal,* August 24, 1984.

185

Police Seize 50 at Slater Park in Crackdown on Drug Traffic

By Tom Drury
Journal-Bulletin Staff Writer

PAWTUCKET—Police raided a parking lot in Slater Park last night, bringing 50 people in for arrest or questioning after a five-week undercover investigation into the allegedly flourishing drug trade near the duck pond.

After police converged on the lot, sealing the entrance and exit with marked cruisers at about 7 P.M., 10 adults were jailed for arraignment this morning on a variety of drug charges, police said.

Of 23 adults who were released, eight may be charged depending on the results of toxicologists' examination of seized substances and tablets, according to Lt. Ted Dolan, head of the Special Squad. In addition, he said, police are still holding seven unserved arrest warrants stemming from the investigation.

Seventeen minors were also brought in for questioning. Dolan said seven of them may be charged in Family Court, two for drug sales to an undercover officer.

The raid, which followed a series of a dozen purchases of marijuana, cocaine, or PCP, by undercover officers from East Providence and Lincoln, was attended by Mayor and Public Safety Director Henry S. Kinch and Police Chief Joseph C. Roy.

"We were satisfied," Dolan said. "We think we've put an end to the narcotic problem at Slater Park. Now for how long, I don't know."

Dolan said 20 officers conducted the raid, pouring out of police vans and walking up through the woods to prevent escape. He said they met little resistance but did run into an angry pit bull leashed to the bumper of one suspect's car.

The dog "was foaming at the mouth," Dolan said.

"We took him and secured him inside the automobile
and had a family member respond to the scene and
take him home."

"We had the defendant put him in the car," Dolan
said, clarifying. "My mother didn't raise any fools."

Dolan said the investigation and raid stemmed
from numerous complaints about street sales in the
area, and that police seized relatively small amounts
of drugs: small amounts of cocaine, PCP and marijuana, "a pound of grass here, a half ounce of coke
there."

The article then lists the name, address, age, and charge
against each of the ten people.

Now, a little more is to be noticed here than might at first
strike one's awareness. For the first several paragraphs it
is almost impossible to read this without concentrating on
the facts that are coming out—and that is as it is supposed
to be. The account is absolutely straightforward, flat, and
the mind tends to focus on those facts so directly that one
may not even be aware that he is *reading*. The writer has
created that transparent window between the reader and
the facts, and even while following a written account, he
may be hardly aware of that. It thus seems that rare speci-
men: a perfect example of writing that has no discernible
style at all.

But is that all there is to it? No. Lieutenant Ted Dolan has
volunteered to the reporter that the police were satisfied,
and he also mentions that they had no trouble except for
"an angry pit bull leashed to the bumper of one suspect's
car." The reporter duly notes the lieutenant's lapse into
policese: the dog "was foaming at the mouth," but they
"secured" him inside the automobile, had a family member
"respond to the scene" and had "the defendant" put him in
the car. Then the lieutenant says, "My mother didn't raise
any fools."

If your response at this point is to think, "Wait a minute," then you have just discovered that this piece not only does have a style, it has a very effective style. If Mrs. Dolan didn't raise any fools, then what were all those grown men doing there chasing around a duck pond arresting a bunch of kids on a pot bust that took five weeks of police time to organize? Will it stop the drug traffic? No. Wasn't the main purpose not to arrest young people who will undoubtedly be back on the street in a day or two at most, but to give the mayor and the police some publicity? Of course. So the whole enterprise is a charade staged strictly for the benefit of the newspaper account that will come from it and, if they are lucky, from the TV news report that will be on everyone's screen the next day. And as for Dolan's canny mother, didn't she teach young Ted that a dog actually foams at the mouth only if it has rabies, and if there is a rabid dog in Pawtucket, then that fact will be on the front page of every newspaper in New England the very next day? If Ted is scared of a leashed dog that is barking because it is leashed and thinks the beast is far more dangerous than it is, then what did Mrs. Dolan raise?

What we actually have here is a lovely example of a very American sort of humor. It is a kind of social satire that is wry and unassuming, but it has a long pedigree and has been used by some genuine American masters, among them Thomas Chandler Haliburton, Mark Twain, and Ring Lardner. The style, of course, stems not so much from *how* the story is told, for that is utterly deadpan, but from *what* is included. The reporter never stops being the dutiful reporter, putting in what the lieutenant tells him and getting it exactly right. It's just a question of what he decides to include in the story.

One touch that the connoisseur should not fail to pick up comes with " 'We had the defendant put him in the car,' Dolan said, clarifying." *Clarifying?* That word puts the sentence directly in a splendid American tradition best exemplified by Ring Lardner's immortal line, " 'Shut up,' he explained." A small point, perhaps, but then writing is made up of small points.

There has been a great deal of talk in serious critical circles about the absence of overt style, and a number of our best writers have professed to write in it, George Orwell prominent among them. Such protestations, though, carry little weight. Orwell writes very well and does indeed avoid self-conscious mannerisms, so that the result reads much like a good newspaper account, but to think that this means that he has no style is to mistake him entirely. His is a very controlled style that does not get in the way, but with Orwell there is never any doubt as to who is speaking. As a novelist he seems to me very hard to read since he has no ability to breathe life into his characters, but his good things, like *Down and Out in Paris and London*, *Shooting an Elephant,* and *Such, Such, Were the Joys,* all openly autobiographical, are brilliant and passionate and scarifying. If an aspiring writer were to ask me what modern author would best serve as a guide to the formation of a style, I would always recommend Orwell.

When I was young, those of us who had given serious thought to the idea of becoming writers all felt that each writer had to develop an individual style, a *voice* that would be unmistakably his own. We had no interest in the idea that the writing should be as unobtrusive as possible—quite the contrary. Looking around, we saw that all the most admired writers had a strong individual style and that the very distinctiveness of their style helped to make them so famous. Hemingway and Faulkner were the giants of the time and each had a style that was almost overwhelming, but we felt that if we had been handed passages by Steinbeck, O'Hara, or Maugham we should have been able to identify their author from the style of the piece alone. I was never able to do that, but some who read *The Talk of the Town* in *The New Yorker* every week were able to identify the authors of the unsigned pieces—or at least they claimed they could.

The trouble with this was that some people who could have become perfectly good writers never did, for by trying for effect they shut off the possibility of getting their ideas across. The search for a style became nothing but an impediment in the road. They had not stopped to remind themselves that writing is communication and that anything that impedes clean communication is to be avoided. The readers of this book should remember that style creeps in quite unconsciously as a writer's prose comes to reflect his inner mind—in fact, one cannot write in the "no style" style if he wanted to. The point is this: it is better to try to write as directly and openly as possible and without any attempt at effect, and then the rest will take care of itself.

And does style matter? Indeed it does. To show a few examples, I have picked up a few quotes from various book reviews.

Here is Rodger Doyle writing in the *New York Times Book Review* on April 3, 1988, about John Elkington's *The Poisoned Womb: Human Reproduction in a Polluted World:*

> Few environmental issues inspire more anxiety than the effect of synthetic chemicals on the unborn. . . . Some 25,000 synthetic chemicals are widely used in commerce, but we know little about the toxicity of most of these to reproduction. [This book] attempts to cover this ground for the nonspecialist. . . .
>
> But this book is unsatisfying partly because so little conclusive research has been done on the subject and partly because of Mr. Elkington's flat style. Those in need of a concise summary of the risk in their own industry will look in vain, while those interested in examining the original research studies will be frustrated by haphazard citation of the literature. Mr. Elkington's book may be timely, but it is unlikely to move people to action in the way that Rachel Carson's vivid, hypnotic account of the danger of pesticides did in "Silent Spring."

A review such as this, of course, kills the sale of a book, so the publisher is crushed by it and the author is no doubt indignant. But style is at the root of the trouble.

In the *London Review of Books* (May 5, 1988), John Lanchester wrote on the subject of John Updike and his new book *S.: A Novel.*

> Is it possible for a novelist to write too well? This has sometimes seemed to be the case with John Updike, whose ability to evoke physical detail is unmatched. It is a virtue in accordance with his expressedly realist aesthetic. "My own style seemed to be a groping and elemental attempt to approximate the complexity of envisioned phenomena, and it surprised me to have it called luxuriant and self-indulgent; self-indulgent, surely, is what it wasn't—*other*-indulgent, rather. My models were the styles of Proust and Henry Green as I read them (one in translation): styles of tender exploration that tried to wrap themselves around the things, the tints and voices and perfumes, of the apprehended real." The words that stand out in Updike's description of what he is up to are "groping and elemental." No one in their right mind would ever use either term to describe Updike's prose, whose most striking characteristic is its evenness of texture and never faltering fluency. It's this evenness of texture that is the basis for the charge that he writes too well.

If it is any consolation to the readers of this book, I should confess that Updike's virtues have never been apparent to me. I think his writing is arch, self-conscious, and mannered. I have also repeatedly been a failure in my attempts to be a fiction editor, which is why I stopped publishing fiction many years ago. Updike is one of our most esteemed and successful novelists, placed on the same level as Nabokov by literary circles and almost as beloved of his publisher and banker as Sidney Sheldon. He is, in fact, that very rare instance in American artistic life, a man who is a success both critically and financially. Who am I to criticize the man?

But what about style not being what the man writes but it being what the man is? My parents thought that George Santayana was a great philosopher, and his books hung around the house for years. I tried to read them and found that I couldn't—another instance of my unrefined taste— and then, finally, was somewhat pleased to read a recent reassessment of the man. In the course of writing a long review of *The Sense of Santayana* in the *New York Review of Books* (March 31, 1988), Jonathan Lieberson, first hinting that the attempt to revive Santayana's reputation was destined to fail because he was not in fact a great thinker, then adds:

> Nor is he a great writer, as so many have urged. It is true that the atmosphere pervading his work is beautiful and cold. But everything that he writes is so barnacled with literary effect, so packed with portentous implication, so multiply allusive, that it is often impossible to make out what he is saying without having to reread him. His prose calls too much attention to itself; it produces a kind of purple philosophy, fussy and overembellished, as when he writes such things as "nature is drawn like a sponge, heavy and dripping, from the waters of sentience." Aldous Huxley observed that the "exquisitely good writing" of Santayana is "only another kind of bad writing."[1] It has the quality that you can read it again and again without quite following it and yet at the same time feeling both impressed by it and increasingly cloyed. There is a good deal to what C.S. Peirce wrote in a review of *The Life of Reason*.[2] Santayana's style,

he said, is "highly polished, in a medium more glittering than lucid."

[1]Quoted in Cyril Connolly, *The Evening Colonnade* (Harcourt Brace Jovanovich, 1985), p. 245.

[2]*The Nation* (June 8, 1905).

Style thus segues into and imperceptibly becomes substance as it comes to reflect the inner being of the writer. The beginner need think nothing about it, and even the more practiced writer should hold down any tendency to produce flourishes and call attention to what he is doing, for style will come of itself with enough practice and as a body of work builds up over a period of years.

Style, however, is of the essence in several forms of writing, and thus we will take a quick look at some of them, even though I do not feel that they are the proper subject of this book. Poetry, business and technical writing, and humor depend less for their effect on substance than on the manner in which they are done, so style is more important to these genres than to the kinds of writing we have so far been thinking about. The student should not attempt any of these genres until he has a firm grounding in the more direct and workaday types of writing. Nonetheless, we shall take a look at them for the instruction they do provide.

POETRY

POETRY IS, OF COURSE, VERY ANCIENT. The form was first used as a mnemonic device, for lines that have a recognizable cadence or rhythm and whose lines end in rhymes are much easier to remember than straight narrative. Thus such great events as the Trojan War that were enshrined in folk memory were cast in verse and recited as poems. It is easier to spot an error in a poem than it is in prose, and the reinforcing effect of the beat and the rhymes together are very strong. Almost all of the great "culture memory" pieces of antiquity are written as poetry, and this tradition lasted until the general use of the printing press greatly lessened the role of memory in the keeping of important cultural memories.

In antiquity, poetry occupied a position equal in importance to sculpture, architecture, and playwriting in the arts, and that position has lasted up until very recent times. Between Sappho in the early sixth century B.C. and Wordsworth, Keats, and Shelley in the early 1800s is a span of some twenty-four hundred years, and in all that time poetry was assumed to be one of the highest and most difficult of the arts, recited upon important public occasions, and learned as the basic intellectual and aesthetic equipment of an educated person. Anyone aspiring to become a writer would as a matter of course practice writing poems, for they were thought to be the best teachers of order, discipline, and sensibility. To learn how to write an acceptable poem was to learn how to create art.

Today all that has changed. In the past seventy-five or hundred years poetry has declined from a high, noble art to become the province of small-time academics elbowing each other for forgettable prizes and appointments at second-rate universities. It has lost its importance and completely lost its audience. The publishing world, incredibly tradition-minded and conservative, still prints reams of poetry, but nobody buys it or reads it. In any given year dozens of volumes of poetry are announced in *Publishers Weekly,* which means that they were done by real publishers with a real expectation of bookstore and library sales. Many other volumes of poetry were printed by small presses and private publishers that had no real expectation of sale, so the total is actually much larger, and virtually none of these volumes sold enough copies to justify its publication on commercial grounds.

In our time a poet will occasionally break through the general fog of indifference that surrounds the genre to become a celebrity, sometimes by scandalous behavior. And by achieving celebrity status he himself becomes an object of interest and thus gets his poems read. Dylan Thomas is the defining modern case.

It is true that the World War I poets and T. S. Eliot, Ezra Pound, and Robert Frost developed real audiences in their time and that serious poets keep on writing and publishers keep on publishing and prize awards committees keep on selecting, but it is also true that as a significant component of modern culture poetry has sunk out of sight. The reasons for this state of affairs are various but could include the incredible rise of all sorts of new forms of communication such as radio, television, movies, and recordings of music to compete with the older forms, the breakdown in the community of educated people from a small and serious elite into a huge and much less well educated mass, and the influence of what might be called modernism on the poets themselves. By modernism I mean that movement in painting that broke down the old realist and representational traditions in art, first with impressionism, then with cubism and so on through to abstract expressionism all the way along to conceptual art, to completely change the nature of the art. The revolution in painting had considerable echoes in poetry, but what may be possible in a visual art is really not possible in writing, for with writing there is no getting away from words. The average viewer of a picture will always try to find a pattern in it, whether it is there or not, but if words don't make sense on their face, then there is nothing to do but leave them alone. Thus painters could abandon the image but writers could not abandon meaning. When they tried, all they did was drive away their readers.

And what does all this mean for an aspiring writer? My answer is that if a person likes poetry its practice is as valuable now as it ever was, but he will only get something worth having if he does it in the formal, classical way. Learning to work within strict forms, finding pleasing rhymes, and constructing a poem as carefully as one would a house have great charms and cannot but help to make for a better writer. It is not easy, and most people aren't willing to do that much work for what seems so little result—but if in a lifetime, a person could compose a single sonnet to equal one of Shakespeare's he could forever after call himself a writer.

BUSINESS AND TECHNICAL WRITING

IN THE COURSE OF HOLDING most any office job, one will from time to time be called upon to write something. This will usually be a report, a proposal, or a presentation to a gathering. The majority of people who try to do this are very unsure of themselves both as writers and as reporters and thus tend to hide behind jargon or what might be called bureaucratese. They also tend to adopt an office or business lexicon full of big words with specialized meanings, and as a result their efforts often become almost entirely impenetrable.

My plea, which can hardly be made too forcefully, is to insist on writing plain English in the office. It cannot be overemphasized that clear thinking and direct and understandable writing is in very short supply in any office, and if a person's writing becomes known for those qualities his career will take a great leap forward. This is absolutely not an idle promise. The person who becomes the office writer soon discovers that how anything is written will subtly but powerfully effect how well taken it is. The writer gets to put forward his proposals before anyone else and can shape the proposals of others to suit his purposes. Let us say that the president of the company is going to a meeting of the national league of whatever-sort-of-business-it-is and asks the writer to get him up a speech. But when the writer asks what he wants to say, the president has only a hazy idea. So the writer than works up a draft for his approval. Whose ideas will end up in the speech? Only those that the writer put forward.

But there is more to it than that because not everyone can become the office writer. Let's say that most of the company's employees are salesmen. One of them is asked to look into and prepare a report on the idea of whether the company should open three new sales offices in the Midwest. Now the salesman, not used to writing at all, is in a bind. He doesn't know how to do a report like that. At this point he should turn to a good textbook, and the one I recommend is *Technical Writing: Situations and Strategies,* by Michael H. Markel.

To write any report it is only necessary to keep a clear head and take a completely objective and direct approach to the question. As to new sales offices, well, first the writer should describe the present situation. Then he should lay out the assorted possibilities for future change, plot the expected results, and assess the costs, the level of risk, and the expectation of benefit. He could add his own recommendation or write the report in such a way that his own position is obvious. He must simply be clear, attacking the problem in logical steps and never letting the politics of the situation intimidate him. As long as he writes with the good of the whole company uppermost in his mind, he will be all right.

Here are some things *not* to do that textbooks don't always mention:

First, the good business writer avoids jargon. His vocabulary does not include *interface, effectuate* or *implement,* or *paradigm.* They are all words that have been used so regularly around offices that they have become passé and stand as examples of how today's jargon becomes tomorrow's out-of-date expressions. Instead he uses *meet, carry out* or *do,* and *example* or *pattern.*

Second, a wise officeworker never writes nasty letters or

puts any criticism in writing. If a person is trapped into putting his criticisms down on paper, they will always come back to haunt him—always. Negative thoughts about anything should come out gently over the lunch table or around the bar after work—that is what business socializing is for—and even then a person has to be very careful indeed. In any case, nothing in writing should be anything but positive.

Third, nothing should be put down in writing that should be kept secret. There are no secrets in an office, and people who try to keep them are always exposed sooner or later. Private matters should be discussed behind closed doors. That is why offices have doors.

Fourth, doing homework is absolutely essential. A businessman needs to think of all the possible questions that could be asked about what he is working on and to have answers ready before the questions come up. That way, he will never get caught flatfooted in an open meeting. He should also always know more than he puts in his report and assume that when he is being asked about his report the questions will be hostile.

Fifth, emotions should never intrude into business writing; it should always be impersonal. The writer should also try to use the active voice ("We decided to . . .") rather than the passive ("It was decided that . . ."). Metaphors, similes, and other tropes are inappropriate, as is cute, apologetic, or humorous prose. And the office writer never tries to upstage his boss.

There are exceptions to everything. In a publishing house, for example, if a book reader's report on a manuscript shows no enthusiasm the book gets rejected, but that is a special case. In general, these rules will keep a novice from harm while he practices how to write clear plain English. While he is doing that, though, he should also remember that it never hurts if he regularly exceeds his sales quota.

HUMOR

FOR OUR PURPOSES, *humor* means anything that is light, occasional, or done merely for the fun of it, and it includes light verse, satire, parody, jokes, games, puzzles, and a lot of other miscellaneous stuff that would be hard to put in other categories. Humor is written by people who have a natural talent for it. I know of no way to learn to write it, but that shouldn't stop anyone from at least attempting it. If people take to it, fine; the writer will then know he has the knack. If people are merely polite, however, he should turn to another genre.

In every period, people seem to feel that humor has fallen to a new low and is in poor shape. It certainly seems that way now. Except for Lake Wobegone and Garrison Keillor, who is writing in a classic American tradition, all that is in view is cat cartoons. Television humor consists chiefly of insults, and magazine humor seems to be dominated by schoolboys who have just discovered bathroom jokes. Perhaps it was ever thus, but I do think that the 1920s, say, were a better time for humor. People forget it, but Harold Ross of *The New Yorker* was a rube—the very essence of a yokel—so he saw inflated egos and pompous attitudes for what they were and delighted in running parodies and put-downs of them. Looking at the humor of Robert Benchley and James Thurber, both of whom contributed to *The New*

Yorker, we can see how very innocent it really was. Today, however, everybody is a cynic. I suppose that is just what they were saying in about 120 B.C., sixty years after Plautus had died, but there you are.

One tiny corner of the field that always especially attracted me, and one in which I published with much pleasure, is wordplay. *An Almanac of Words at Play,* by Willard R. Espy, was perhaps the most characteristic of this type of book. I recommend such things to aspiring writers because I think that playing with words can only improve a writer's technique. If people who aspire to be writers hate wordplay, I am always a little suspicious. Words are the tools of the trade, and I think it natural for a writer to enjoy them for their own sake. The early works of Shakespeare contained a lot of wordplay, and that always seemed to me to be very significant. In any case always keep in mind my basic rule of life: if it isn't fun, the hell with it.

But after all that we cannot leave questions of style without a few lollipops. Here are some examples that I consider high style and very much admire.

George Bernard Shaw was a great man. Whether he was a great playwright is not for me to say, but Professor Higgins and Eliza Doolittle are likely to remain stage favorites for a long time, and in his time Shaw was certainly one of the great writers about the stage. For me, though, he is at his most forceful and pungent in his letters, for they are his most uncalculated utterances, poured out on a daily basis over the many years of his very long life. In them he goes directly to what he has to say without a single wasted word, stripping away all pleasantries and banalities.

One of Shaw's correspondents was Molly Tompkins, a young American actress who managed to get him to notice her, convincing him that she wanted to learn how to be a Shavian actress. In his significant correspondence with her, which was collected by Peter Tompkins in *To a Young Actress: The Letters of Bernard Shaw to Molly Tompkins,* he gave her all his best advice. Here, in his first letter to her, he discusses learning to speak for the stage:

27th December 1921.

My dear Mollytompkins

. . . Now I will tell you something about your little performance. I do not think you have much to learn that can be taught in school by an ordinary teacher. You will have to acquire the English alphabet in Gower St : you still have very queer Rs from the cockney standpoint, and one or two other letters that will bear polishing. Dont pick up smart English, which is bad English : all you need do is to drop certain provincialisms. However your Welsh instructor will take care of that " University College is not Oxford, thank heaven ! For the rest, what you want is work, or rather sheer drudgery to put up your muscle, and give you the hard driven professional touch that comes from doing a thing every day for ten years and in no other way. Without that, although you may know how a thing should be done, and understand it a thousand times better than a hack fifty-dollar-a-week actress, she will "get it across" more effectively than you. I dont know whether you are a musician. If not, you dont know Mozart ; and if you dont know Mozart you will never understand my technique. If you are, you must have noticed sometime or another that though a composer may play his music ever so much more beautifully and intelligently than a professional pianist, yet he cannot produce the same effect in a concert room, because he hasnt got the steel in his fingers. You have to get steel in the muscles of your face, and steel in your heart, by hammering away every day (or night) until you can hit the boy at the back of the gallery in a three hundred pound house. Dont think that at present you can reach only three rows of stalls and that as you go on you will carry a row further and yet another row until you get to the wall. That's not it at all. You can reach the boy all right now, just as you can reach the conductor of the band. But you can't take possession of him and hold him up above the discomfort of his cheap seat.

This excellent advice the young actress did not take—but an aspiring writer should.

The most notable stylist of our present time is, I think, Murray Kempton. Like Red Smith before him, he writes for daily newspapers and often manages to sound as if he had thought about a piece a long time before he knocked it out—but he still is able to write day after day in a remarkably ripe manner. He is able to occupy the moral high ground without effort, and the follies and buffooneries so richly presented to the commentator of American life seem to have been served up by a thoughtful providence to the acid notice of his pen. It is, as you can see, a style that tends to be contagious, but I urge the student to resist the temptation to imitate it.

The following extract is from Kempton's discussion of *A Bright Shining Lie: John Paul Vann and America in Vietnam*, by Neil Sheehan, for *The New York Review of Books* (November 24, 1988), which appeared a week before the book received the 1988 National Book Award for nonfiction. Vann had come to notice because when he was in uniform he publicly differed from his superiors by saying the war could not be won, yet when he was later returned to Vietnam as a civilian he changed his mind. Here Kempton speaks of that shift:

> Then Vann acquired the de facto command of the war effort in the highlands and rice paddies of the Central Coast. The machines whose excesses he had deplored as a wicked futility were his to do with as it pleased him now, and when Larry Stern of *The Washington Post* looked him up at Pleiku in June of 1972, his whole person seemed "suffused with rage and exaltation." "Anytime the wind is blowing from the North where the B-52 strikes are turning the

terrain into a moonscape, you can tell from the bat-
tlefield stench that the strikes are effective," Vann
instructed Stern. "Outside Kontum, wherever you
dropped bombs, you scattered bodies."

The death that had so long refused to be his bride
has been delivered to him as his handmaiden; and
she was a bequest in default of contending heirs. The
proconsuls whose superior rank had so long given
them a better title to her services were by now sick
of the enterprise; the United States was packing its
bags; and John Paul Vann might soon be the last old
stager left in this lost colony. Death had become his
to order about because fewer and fewer of his coun-
trymen of weight were still disposed to press their
claim upon a property that was turning out to be as
worthless for advancing a career as it had been for
sustaining a cause.

Sheehan's final words on Vann are: "He died be-
lieving he had won his war."

Because Kempton is so very flamboyant, perhaps we
should look at a style more serene and selfless, and so I
think we need a taste of Rachel Carson. She seems to me to
have been a very important writer, one to whom the entire
ecological movement owes a deep and lasting debt, for it was
with *The Sea Around Us,* published by the Oxford University Press in 1951, that so-called nature writing graduated
from being the province of a dedicated few to the concern
of a large and newly enlightened public. Serious science
writing for the general public was not at that time widely
accepted, and Rachel Carson, largely due to her wonderful
way of writing, was one of the first and most important
people to bridge the gap between the working scientist and
a substantial literate public. Her book marked the start of
what would become a whole movement, not only in the
writing and publishing of books but in the way the American voting public would respond to ecological issues. This is

no place for an extended essay on the climate of opinion in a democratic country and how it changes, but the pivotal position of this one book in influencing public opinion could easily form the basis for a first-rate doctoral thesis at some forward-looking university. But let's listen to Carson:

For the sea as a whole, the alternation of day and night, the passage of the seasons, the procession of the years, are lost in its vastness, obliterated in its own changeless eternity. But the surface waters are different. The face of the sea is always changing. Crossed by colors, lights, and moving shadows, sparkling in the sun, mysterious in the twilight, its aspects and its moods vary hour by hour. The surface waters move with the tides, stir to the breath of the winds, and rise and fall to the endless, hurrying forms of the waves. Most of all, they change with the advance of the seasons. Spring moves over the temperate lands of our Northern Hemisphere in a tide of new life, of pushing green shoots and unfolding buds, all its mysteries and meanings symbolized in the northward migration of the birds, the awakening of sluggish amphibian life as the chorus of frogs rises again from the wetlands, the different sound of the wind which stirs the young leaves where a month ago it rattled the bare branches. These things we associate with the land, and it is easy to suppose that at sea there could be no such feeling of advancing spring. But the signs are there, and seen with understanding eye, they bring the same magical sense of awakening.

In the sea, as on land, spring is a time for the renewal of life. During the long months of winter in the temperate zones the surface waters have been absorbing the cold. Now the heavy water begins to sink, slipping down and displacing the warmer layers below. Rich stores of minerals have been accumulating on the floor of the continental shelf—some freighted down the rivers from the lands; some derived from sea creatures that have died and whose remains have drifted down to the bottom; some from the shells that once encased a diatom, the streaming protoplasm of a radiolarian, or the transparent tissues of a pteropod. Nothing is wasted in the sea; every particle of material is used over and over again, first by one creature then by another. And when in spring the waters are deeply stirred, the warm bottom water brings to the surface a rich supply of minerals, ready for use by new forms of life.

But this book cannot end without a final word from a master. It must be remembered first that the year 1932 was the bottom of the Great Depression. The stock market had crashed in 1929 and had continued going down, so that by 1932 it had lost *90 percent* of its pre-crash value. No one knew or understood what had happened or when it would end, and in this uncertain and desperate year Charles Scribner's Sons badly needed a best-selling book by its leading author, Ernest Hemingway. He had recently taken it into his head to write a book about bullfighting, a cruel and bloody Spanish spectacle that Americans generally knew nothing about and were usually repelled by when they did. Maxwell Perkins, Hemingway's editor, was no exception: his dislike of the subject was matched only by his desire to get it out of the way so that his writer could go on to a big novel. He therefore hurried Hemingway along.

Hemingway, obviously pressed, turned in *Death in the Afternoon* but added to it a quick last chapter as a sort of protest against how hard he was being pushed: "If I could have made this enough of a book it would have had everything in it." Then he goes on to mention some of the things he would have liked to have had a chance to include but didn't: "It should have the smell of burnt powder and the smoke and the flash and the noise of the traca going off through the green leaves of the trees. . . . And why should it not have the cavalry crossing another stream at a ford, the shadow of the leaves on the horses."

It didn't have those things or lots of others, but that image of the horses picking their way across the pebbles of the ford in the stream with the sunlight dappling them with shadows was something that stayed in his mind, and when it came time to end Robert Jordan's life in *For Whom the Bell*

Tolls, which was the book Perkins had been waiting and hoping for all along, Hemingway remembered it. But as he was writing *Death in the Afternoon* Perkins was standing behind him, pressing, and so he went ahead and finished the last chapter:

What else should it contain about a country you love very much? Rafael says things are very changed and he won't go to Pamplona any more. *La Libertad* I find is getting like *La Temps.* It is no longer the paper where you could put a notice and know the pickpocket would see it now that Republicans are all respectable and Pamplona is changed, of course, but not as much as we are older. I found that if you took a drink that it got very much the same as it was always. I know things change now and I do not care. It's all been changed for me. Let it all change. We'll all be gone before it's changed too much and if no deluge comes when we are gone it still will rain in summer in the north and hawks will nest in the Cathedral at Santiago and in La Granja, where we practiced with the cape on the long gravelled paths between the shadows, it makes no difference if the fountains play or not. We never will ride back from Toledo in the dark, washing the dust out with Fundador, nor will there be that week of what happened in the night in that July in Madrid. We've seen it all go and we'll watch it go again. The great thing is to last and get your work done and see and hear and learn and understand; and write when there is something that you know; and not before; and not too damned much after. Let those who want to save the world if you can get to see it clear and as a whole. Then any part you make will represent the whole if it's made truly. The thing to do is work and learn to make it. No. It is not enough of a book, but still there were a few things to be said. There were a few practical things to be said.

And that is the best advice a great writer ever gave to those who would come after him. It does not scan and it will not parse, but it bears the mark of genius, for in spite of its clearly hurried nature it comes from deep within. If it does not say anything to you, then perhaps you lack the soul of a writer. If it gives you a jolt, then all you have to do is remember that however it is expressed, it is what comes from deep within that counts. If you really wish to write, then just bring it up from the lungs, and let it all come out.

APPENDIX I: FICTION

THIS BRIEF LIST is not meant to be exhaustive or authoritative but to give the would-be fiction writer a few useful books with which to begin. There are dozens of books on the history and criticism of fiction and more on fiction techniques, and anyone who finds this list too short should look for other books in *The Subject Guide to Books in Print*. What is listed here, however, has already been found useful by many students.

Cassill, R. V. *Writing Fiction*. 2nd ed. Prentice-Hall Press, 1986.
A well-known novelist and teacher's pithy introduction, much used in writing courses.

Burroway, Janet. *Writing Fiction: A Guide to Narrative Craft*. Little, Brown & Co., 1982.
A standard text with many examples. Very widely used in formal courses.

Forster, E. M. *Aspects of the Novel*. Harcourt, Brace, 1956.
Well known and oft quoted.

Gardner, John. *The Art of Fiction*. Vintage Books edition, 1985.

Gardner, John. *On Becoming a Novelist*. Harper & Row, 1983.
Both of Gardner's books have established themselves as standard fare for the student and are generally admired.

Hale, Nancy. *The Realities of Fiction: A Book about Writing*. Reprinted in 1977 from 1962 ed. Westport, CT: Greenwood.

James, Henry. *The Theory of Fiction.* University of Nebraska Press, 1972.
The master speaks.

Kennedy, X. J. *An Introduction to Fiction.* 3rd ed. Little, Brown, 1983.
A useful standard text.

Kundera, Milan. *The Art of the Novel.* Grove Press, 1987.
Much quoted by critics.

McCormick, Mona. *The Fiction Writer's Research Handbook.* NAL, 1988.
A surprisingly useful guide.

Stevick, Philip, ed. *The Theory of the Novel.* Free Press, 1967.
A durable standard.

Sloane, William. *The Craft of Writing.* Norton, 1979.
A very good editor can only be of help.

Zinsser, William. *On Writing Well.* Harper & Row, 1980.
A basic necessity for every writer.

APPENDIX II: JOURNALISM

THERE ARE SO MANY SCHOOLS OF JOURNALISM and so many courses in writing that they would be impossible to list here. The following three sources are very useful places to start if the student is looking for formal courses. It should be remembered, though, that one does not have to take a set of formal courses to learn something. Most colleges and universities have some sort of extension or adult education section and offer a variety of evening courses or seminars that can be very useful. Before embarking on a possibly distant and expensive enrollment, the student should check with local centers of learning to see what they offer. Otherwise, these sources will lead to what is available throughout the country.

Guide to American Graduate Schools. Livesey and Gene A. Robbins. Viking Press, 1970.
This covers forty-seven journalism programs.

Peterson's Graduate and Professional Programs: An Overview, 1987. 21st ed. Series editor: Amy J. Goldstein; data editor: Raymond D. Sacchetti.
The annual Peterson's guides are basic, and the latest should be consulted. This edition lists seventy-nine journalism programs and ninety-three writing programs and seems the most comprehensive available.

Occupational Outlook Handbook, 1988–89. U.S. Dept. of Labor, April 1988, Bulletin 2300.
This would be easy to miss but can be very helpful. It should be available in any public library.

211

BIBLIOGRAPHY

Adair, Robert K. *The Great Design: Particles, Fields, and Creation.* Oxford University Press, 1987.

Alexander, Edwin P. *Down at the Depot: American Railroad Stations from 1831 to 1920.* Clarkson N. Potter, 1970.

Anderson, Nancy Scott, and Dwight Anderson. *The Generals: Ulysses S. Grant and Robert E. Lee.* Alfred A. Knopf, 1988.

Bertholle, Louisette. *French Cuisine for All.* Doubleday, 1980.

Burt, Alison. *The Gourmet's Guide to French Cooking.* Octopus Books Ltd., 1973.

Carnegie, Dale. *How to Win Friends and Influence People.* Rev. Ed. Pocket Books, 1983.

Caro, Robert A. *The Path to Power: The Years of Lyndon Johnson.* Alfred A. Knopf, 1982.

———. *The Power Broker.* Random House, 1975.

Carson, Rachel. *Silent Spring.* Oxford University Press, 1962.

———. *The Sea Around Us.* Oxford University Press, 1951.

Catton, Bruce. *This Hallowed Ground: The Story of the Union Side of the Civil War.* Doubleday, 1956.

———. *Mr. Lincoln's Army.* Doubleday, 1953.

Chandler, David Leon. *Henry Flagler.* Macmillan, 1986.

Child, Julia, Louisette Bertholle, and Simone Beck. *Mastering the Art of French Cooking.* 2 vols. Alfred A. Knopf, 1966, 1970.

Clausewitz, Karl von. *On War.* Reprint. Princeton University Press, 1976.

Cunningham, Noble E., Jr. *In Pursuit of Reason: The Life of Thomas Jefferson.* Louisiana State University Press, 1987.

Dalzell, Robert F., Jr. *Enterprising Elite: The Boston Associates and the World They Made.* Harvard University Press, 1987.

Dana, Nathalie. *Young in New York.* Doubleday, 1962.

Dryfhout, John H. *The Work of Augustus Saint-Gaudens.* University Press of New England, 1982.

Elisofon, Eliot. *Java Diary.* Macmillan, 1969.

Elkington, John. *The Poisoned Womb: Human Reproduction in a Polluted World.* Penguin, 1988.

Espy, Willard R. *An Almanac of Words at Play.* Clarkson N. Potter, 1975.

Fitzgerald, Frances. *America Revised.* Atlantic-Little, Brown, 1979.

Fontaine, Andre, and William A. Glavin, Jr. *The Art of Writing Nonfiction.* Rev. Ed. Syracuse University Press, 1987.

Ford, Alice, ed. *Audubon, by Himself: A Profile of John James Audubon.* Natural History Press, 1969.

Frank, Anne. *Anne Frank: The Diary of a Young Girl.* Doubleday, 1959.

Gibbon, Edward. *The History of the Decline and Fall of the Roman Empire.* 6 Vols. 1776–1788. One Vol. Abridgement. Penguin, 1983.

The Gourmet Cookbook. Gourmet Magazine, 1950.

Gutman, Herbert. *Power and Culture: Essays on the American Working Class.* Pantheon Books, 1988.

Hawking, Stephen W. *A Brief History of Time: From the Big Bang to Black Holes.* Bantam, 1989.

Hobsbawn, E. J. *The Age of Empire, 1875–1914.* Pantheon Books, 1988.

Jackson, Stanley. *J. P. Morgan.* Stein & Day, 1983.

James, Will. *Smoky.* Scribner's, 1926, 1929.

Kagan, Donald. *The Fall of the Athenian Empire.* Cornell University Press, 1988.

Kennedy, Paul. *The Rise and Fall of the Great Powers: Economic Change and Military Conflict from 1500 to 2000.* Random House, 1987.

Larousse Gastronomique. English edition. Hamlyn, 1961.

Mahan, Alfred T. *The Influence of Sea Power upon History.* Little, Brown, 1890.

Markel, Michael H. *Technical Writing: Situations and Strategies.* St. Martin's Press, 1984.

Maugham, W. Somerset. *A Writer's Notebook.* Doubleday, 1949.

McPherson, James M. *Battle Cry of Freedom: The Civil War Era.* Oxford University Press, 1988.

Morehead, O. F., ed. *Everybody's Pepys: The Diary of Samuel Pepys, 1660–1669.* Harcourt, Brace, 1926.

Nabokov, Vladimir. *Speak, Memory.* Rev. Ed. Putnam's, 1966.

Neumann, John von, and Oskar Morgenstern. *Theory of Games and Economic Behavior.* Princeton University Press, 1944.

Nevins, Allan, ed. *The Diary of Philip Hone, 1828–1851.* Dodd, Mead, 1936.

Orwell, George. *Down and Out in Paris and London.* Harcourt, Brace, 1972.

———. "Such, Such Were the Joys." In *The Collected Essays, Journalism, and Letters.* Harcourt Brace Jovanovitch, 1983.

———. *Shooting an Elephant,* Harcourt Brace Jovanovitch, 1956.

Pagels, Heinz R. *Perfect Symmetry: The Search for the Beginning of Time.* Simon & Schuster, 1985.

Peale, Norman Vincent. *The Power of Positive Thinking.* Reprint. Prentice-Hall, 1954.

Pelikan, Jaroslav. *The Excellent Empire: The Fall of Rome and the Triumph of the Church.* Harper & Row, 1988.

Pierce, John R. *Electronics: Waves and Messages.* Doubleday, 1956.

Plutarch's Lives. John Dryden, trans. Modern Library, 1967.

Prescott, Orville, ed. *History as Literature.* Harper & Row, 1970.

Rombauer, Irma S., and Marion Rombauer Becker. *The Joy of Cooking.* Bobbs-Merrill, 1931.

Shannon, Claude E., and Warren Weaver. *The Mathematical Theory of Communication.* University of Illinois Press, 1949.

Sheehan, Neil. *A Bright Shining Lie: John Paul Vann and America in Vietnam.* Random House, 1988.

Smith, John (Captain). *A Sea Grammar.* 1627. Reprint. London: Michael Joseph, 1970.

Smith, Page. *John Adams.* 2 Vols. McGraw-Hill, 1959.

———. *A People's History of the United States.* 8 Vols. McGraw-Hill, 1987.

Steffens, Lincoln. *The Autobiography of Lincoln Steffens.* Harcourt, Brace, 1931.

Strachey, Lytton. *Eminent Victorians.* Putnam's, 1918.

Tompkins, Peter, ed. *To a Young Actress: The Letters of Bernard Shaw to Molly Tompkins*. Clarkson N. Potter, 1960.

Toynbee, Arnold J. *Mankind and Mother Earth: A Narrative History of the World*. Oxford University Press, 1976.

——. *A Study of History*. Oxford University Press, 1954.

Trefil, James. *The Dark Side of the Universe*. Scribner's, 1988.

Turner, Frederick Jackson. *The Significance of the Frontier in American History*. Silver Buckle Press, 1984.

Updike, John. *S: A Novel*. Knopf, 1988.

Yeager, Chuck, and Leo Janos. *Yeager: An Autobiography*. Bantam, 1985.

COPYRIGHT ACKNOWLEDGMENTS